Measuring Student Knowledge and Skills

THE PISA 2000 ASSESSMENT OF READING, MATHEMATICAL AND SCIENTIFIC LITERACY

OECD

ORGANISATION FOR ECONOMIC CO-OPERATION AND DEVELOPMENT

ORGANISATION FOR ECONOMIC CO-OPERATION
AND DEVELOPMENT

Pursuant to Article 1 of the Convention signed in Paris on 14th December 1960, and which came into force on 30th September 1961, the Organisation for Economic Co-operation and Development (OECD) shall promote policies designed:

- to achieve the highest sustainable economic growth and employment and a rising standard of living in Member countries, while maintaining financial stability, and thus to contribute to the development of the world economy;

- to contribute to sound economic expansion in Member as well as non-member countries in the process of economic development; and

- to contribute to the expansion of world trade on a multilateral, non-discriminatory basis in accordance with international obligations.

The original Member countries of the OECD are Austria, Belgium, Canada, Denmark, France, Germany, Greece, Iceland, Ireland, Italy, Luxembourg, the Netherlands, Norway, Portugal, Spain, Sweden, Switzerland, Turkey, the United Kingdom and the United States. The following countries became Members subsequently through accession at the dates indicated hereafter: Japan (28th April 1964), Finland (28th January 1969), Australia (7th June 1971), New Zealand (29th May 1973), Mexico (18th May 1994), the Czech Republic (21st December 1995), Hungary (7th May 1996), Poland (22nd November 1996) and Korea (12th December 1996). The Commission of the European Communities takes part in the work of the OECD (Article 13 of the OECD Convention).

Publié en français sous le titre:
MESURER LES CONNAISSANCES ET LES COMPÉTENCES DES ÉLÈVES
Lecture, mathématiques et science : l'évaluation de PISA 2000

MEASURING STUDENT KNOWLEDGE AND SKILLS

The PISA 2000 Assessment of Reading, Mathematical and Scientific Literacy

Foreword

How well are young adults prepared to meet the challenges of the future? Are they able to analyse, reason and communicate their ideas effectively? Do they have the capacity to continue learning throughout life? Parents, students, the public and those who run education systems need to know the answers to these questions.

Many education systems monitor student learning to provide some answers to these questions. Comparative international analyses can extend and enrich the national picture by providing a larger context within which to interpret national results. They can provide direction for schools' instructional efforts and for students' learning as well as insights into curriculum strengths and weaknesses. Coupled with appropriate incentives, they can motivate students to learn better, teachers to teach better and schools to be more effective. They also provide tools to allow central authorities to monitor achievement levels even when administration is devolved and schools are run in partnership with communities.

For these reasons, governments and the general public need solid and internationally comparable evidence on educational outcomes. In response to this demand, the OECD has launched the Programme for International Student Assessment (PISA). PISA represents a new commitment by the governments of OECD countries to monitor the outcomes of education systems in terms of student achievement on a regular basis and within a common framework that is internationally agreed. PISA aims at providing a new basis for policy dialogue and for collaboration in defining and operationalising educational goals – in innovative ways that reflect judgements about the skills that are relevant to adult life. It provides inputs for standard-setting and evaluation; insights into the mix of factors which contribute to the development of competencies, and how these factors operate similarly or differently among countries; and a better understanding of the causes and consequences of observed skill gaps. In supporting a shift in policy focus from the inputs used in education systems and institutions to learning outcomes, PISA can assist countries in seeking to bring about improvements in schooling and better preparation for young people as they enter an adult life of rapid change and deepening global interdependence.

PISA is a collaborative effort, bringing together scientific expertise from the participating countries, steered jointly by their governments on the basis of shared, policy-driven interests. Participating countries take responsibility for the project at the policy level. Experts from participating countries also serve on working groups that are charged with linking the PISA policy objectives with the best available substantive and technical expertise in the field of international comparative assessment of educational outcomes. Through participating in these expert groups, countries ensure that the PISA assessment instruments are internationally valid and take into account the cultural and curricular contexts of OECD Member countries; have strong measurement properties; and place an emphasis on authenticity and educational validity. The frameworks and assessment instruments for PISA 2000 are the product of a multi-year development process and were adopted in December 1999 by OECD governments, through the Board of Participating Countries which manages the PISA project.

The PISA 2000 Assessment of Reading, Mathematical and Scientific Literacy is the second volume in the PISA series *Measuring Student Knowledge and Skills*. It introduces the PISA approach to comparative assessment and describes the PISA 2000 assessment instruments in terms of the content that students need to acquire, the processes that need to be performed, and the contexts in which knowledge and skills are applied. Each of the assessment domains is illustrated with a range of sample items. It is published on the responsibility of the Secretary-General of the OECD.

Acknowledgements

This publication was prepared by the Statistics and Indicators Division of the OECD Directorate for Education, Employment, Labour and Social Affairs, principally Andreas Schleicher and Claudia Tamassia. The sample assessment materials presented in this publication were developed by international expert panels and the test developers of the PISA consortium under the direction of Raymond Adams from the Australian Council of Educational Research. The reading expert panel was chaired by Dr. Irwin Kirsch of the Education Testing Service in the United States, the mathematics expert panel was chaired by Professor Jan de Lange from the University of Utrecht, and the science expert panel was chaired by Professor Wynne Harlen from the Scottish Council for Research in Education. Dr. Geoff Masters from the Australian Council for Educational Research prepared the review of the PISA literacy concept in the publication. The members of the expert panels and the PISA test developers are listed in the appendices.

TABLE OF CONTENTS

Introduction

The Programme for International Student Assessment

The OECD's Programme for International Student Assessment (PISA) is a new, regular survey of 15-year-olds which assesses aspects of their preparedness for adult life. The first round of the survey is taking place in 32 countries during 2000, in collaboration between governments and the OECD. Between 4 500 and 10 000 students will be surveyed in each country.

This publication explains the conceptual framework on which the PISA 2000 assessment is based in terms of the content that students need to acquire, the processes that need to be performed, and the contexts in which knowledge and skills are applied. It also illustrates how the assessment is to be performed by reproducing sample assessment items and explaining what each is measuring.

PISA bases its assessment of student outcomes on three domains of "literacy" – reading literacy, mathematical literacy and scientific literacy. In each case, international experts from OECD Member countries have agreed on definitions of literacy and a framework for assessing it, using a common set of principles (OECD, 1999).

The PISA concept of literacy is much wider than the historical notion of the ability to read and write. Common usage now accepts that a literate person has a range of competencies. Moreover, it has come to be accepted that there is no single cut-off point between a person who is fully literate and one who is illiterate. Literacy is measured on a continuum, not as something that one either does or does not have. In PISA, literacy is regarded as knowledge and skills for adult life. Its acquisition is a lifelong process – taking place not just at school or through formal learning, but also through interaction with peers, colleagues and wider communities. Fifteen-year-olds cannot be expected to have learned in school everything that they will need to know as adults. They need a solid foundation of knowledge in areas such as reading, mathematics and science. However, in order to go on learning in these domains and to apply their learning to the real world, they need to understand some basic processes and principles, and have the flexibility to use them in different situations. The three PISA domains of literacy therefore emphasise the ability to undertake a number of fundamental processes in a range of situations, backed by a broad understanding of key concepts, rather than the possession of specific knowledge.

The countries participating in the first OECD/PISA survey cycle are: Australia, Austria, Belgium, Brazil, Canada, China, the Czech Republic, Denmark, Finland, France, Germany, Greece, Hungary, Iceland, Ireland, Italy, Japan, Korea, Latvia, Luxembourg, Mexico, the Netherlands, New Zealand, Norway, Poland, Portugal, the Russian Federation, Spain, Sweden, Switzerland, the United Kingdom and the United States.

BOX 1. WHAT IS OECD/PISA?
A SUMMARY OF KEY FEATURES

Basics

- An internationally standardised assessment, jointly developed by participating countries and administered to 15-year-olds in groups in their schools.

- Administered in 32 countries, of which 28 are members of the OECD.

- Between 4 500 and 10 000 students will typically be tested in each country.

Content

- PISA covers three domains: reading literacy, mathematical literacy and scientific literacy.

- PISA aims to define each domain not merely in terms of mastery of the school curriculum, but in terms of important knowledge and skills needed in adult life. The assessment of cross-curriculum competencies is an integral part of PISA.

- Emphasis is placed on the mastery of processes, the understanding of concepts and the ability to function in various situations within each domain.

Methods

- Pencil and paper tests are used, with assessments lasting a total of 2 hours for each student.

- Test items are a mixture of multiple-choice test items and questions requiring students to construct their own responses. The items are organised in units based on a passage setting out a real-life situation.

- A total of about 7 hours of test items is included, with different students taking different combinations of the test items.

- Students answer a background questionnaire which takes 20-30 minutes to complete, providing information about themselves. School principals are given a 30-minute questionnaire asking about their schools.

Assessment cycle

- The first assessment is taking place in 2000, with first results published in 2001, and will continue thereafter in three-year cycles.

- Each cycle looks in depth at a "major" domain, to which two-thirds of testing time are devoted; the other two domains provide a summary profile of skills. Major domains are reading literacy in 2000, mathematical literacy in 2003 and scientific literacy in 2006.

Outcomes

- A basic profile of knowledge and skills among students at the end of compulsory schooling.

- Contextual indicators relating results to student and school characteristics.

- Trend indicators showing how results change over time.

- A knowledge base for policy analysis and research.

The choice of assessment domains

It has long been accepted that an important objective of schooling is the development of a "literate" adult population. Historically, this objective has been synonymous with ensuring that all adults in a society are able to read and write. Literacy – defined as the ability to read and write – has been seen as essential to personal fulfilment; full adult participation in social, cultural and political life; personal empowerment; and success in securing and maintaining employment.

The notion that schools have a responsibility to create a future society in which all adults are also mathematically "literate", scientifically "literate", and technologically "literate" is a relatively recent idea. For much of the past century, the content of school mathematics and science curricula was dominated by the need to provide foundations for the professional training of mathematicians, scientists and engineers.

But with the increasing role of science, mathematics and technology in modern life, the objectives of personal fulfilment, employment, and full participation in society increasingly require an adult population which is not only able to read and write, but also mathematically, scientifically and technologically literate. In the words of one commentator, "because of its pervasive role in modern society, science is far too important to be left to the scientists only" (Zen, 1992, p. 20).

The imperatives in modern society to develop a citizenry which is mathematically, scientifically and technologically "literate" are very similar to past arguments for achieving basic levels of adult reading and writing competence: "A shared scientific background is part of a common cultural base that binds civilised people together" (Zen, 1992); "Individuals who are deprived of the capacity to make informed choices are rendered more vulnerable in matters of health and environment, and are impaired in their ability to cope with an increasingly technological world" (Galbraith *et al.*, 1997); and basic mathematical and scientific literacy "renders individuals less dependent on others, so that democratic processes, social values, and individual opportunities do not come to be dominated by knowledgeable élites" (Krugly-Smolska, 1990).

Beyond content

A key feature of the broadened definition of "literacy" in PISA is a more explicit focus on the knowledge, understanding and skills required for effective functioning in everyday life.

Literacy for effective participation in modern society requires mastery of a body of basic knowledge and skills. For example, reading literacy depends on the ability to decode text, to interpret meanings of words and grammatical structures, and to construct meaning at least at a superficial level. But reading literacy for effective participation in modern society requires much more than this: it also depends on the ability to read between the lines and to reflect on the purposes and intended audiences of texts, to recognise devices used by writers to convey messages and influence readers, and the ability to interpret meaning from the structures and features of texts. Reading literacy depends on an ability to understand and interpret a wide variety of text types, and to make sense of texts by relating them to the contexts in which they appear.

Mathematical literacy similarly depends on familiarity with a body of mathematical knowledge and skills which includes: basic number facts and operations; working with money; fundamental ideas about space and shape, including working with measurements; and notions of uncertainty, growth and change. But mathematical literacy for effective functioning in modern society requires much more than this: it also depends on the ability to think and work mathematically, including modelling and problem solving. These competencies include knowing the extent and limits of mathematical concepts; following and evaluating mathematical arguments; posing mathematical problems; choosing ways of representing mathematical situations; and expressing oneself on matters with a mathematical content. Mathematical literacy depends on an ability to apply this knowledge, this understanding and these skills in a wide variety of personal, social and work contexts.

Scientific literacy also depends on familiarity with a body of scientific knowledge and skills. This body of knowledge includes an understanding of fundamental scientific concepts such as food chains, sustainability, energy conservation, photosynthesis, rates of reaction, adaptation, states of matter, and inheritance. But scientific literacy for effective functioning in modern society requires much more than this: it also depends on the ability to use processes of scientific enquiry such as recognising the nature and limits of such enquiry; identifying evidence required to answer scientific questions; and drawing, evaluating and communicating conclusions. Scientific literacy depends on an ability to apply this knowledge, this understanding and these skills in a wide variety of personal, social, and work contexts.

OECD/PISA adopts definitions of reading literacy, mathematical literacy and scientific literacy that go beyond mastery of essential knowledge and skills (Box 2). In all three domains, the focus is not primarily on the mastery of specific curriculum content, but on the ability to reflect on and use reading, mathematical and scientific knowledge, understanding and skills to achieve personal goals and to participate effectively in society (OECD, 1999).

BOX 2. OECD/PISA DEFINITIONS OF LITERACY

Reading literacy

The capacity to understand, use and reflect on written texts, in order to achieve one's goals, to develop one's knowledge and potential, and to participate in society.

Mathematical literacy

The capacity to identify, to understand, and to engage in mathematics and make well-founded judgements about the role that mathematics plays, as needed for an individual's current and future private life, occupational life, social life with peers and relatives, and life as a constructive, concerned, and reflective citizen.

Scientific literacy

The capacity to use scientific knowledge, to identify questions and to draw evidence-based conclusions in order to understand and help make decisions about the natural world and the changes made to it through human activity.

Three dimensions of literacy

In each domain, the assessment is organised in three dimensions, corresponding to process skills, knowledge and understanding, and the context of application. The remainder of this chapter gives an overview of each dimension. Chapters 2 to 4 explain more precisely the criteria for assessment in each dimension within individual domains and illustrate these with sample items.

It should be borne in mind that PISA 2000 gives more emphasis to reading literacy than to the other two domains. PISA will take place every three years. In each cycle, two-thirds of testing time will be devoted to assessing one domain in detail. Mathematical literacy will become the major domain in 2003, and scientific literacy in 2006.

Processes

Reading literacy, mathematical literacy and scientific literacy require an understanding of and facility with the methods and processes pertinent to each of these domains.

Beyond the ability to retrieve surface meaning from text, reading literacy requires an understanding and appreciation of the writer's craft, and an ability to reason about text. Readers require an understanding of text structure, genre, and register. They must be able to follow chains of reasoning; to compare and contrast information in a text; draw inferences; identify supporting evidence; identify and understand irony, metaphor and humour; detect nuances and subtleties of language; recognise ways in which texts are constructed to persuade and influence; and relate what they read to their own background experience and knowledge.

> *Although surface understanding is important, it is not enough. In school and in society, we expect a reader to be able to analyse, evaluate, and extend the ideas that are presented, just as we expect a writer to elaborate upon and defend judgements that are expressed. We expect people to know how to get information and to know how to use it and shape it to suit their needs. For example, readers must learn to relate what they are reading to their personal experience in order to integrate new ideas with what they know — perhaps modifying or rejecting the ideas in the process of considering them more fully. Readers must also learn to test the validity of what they read by comparing it with information from other sources, as well as to judge the internal logic and consistency of the ideas and information presented (Applebee* et al., *1987, p. 9).*

Mathematical literacy similarly involves a range of process skills. The focus here is on students' abilities to analyse, reason and communicate ideas effectively by posing, formulating and solving mathematical problems. Mathematical literacy skills include thinking skills (e.g., distinguishing between different kinds of mathematical statements); argumentation skills (e.g., following and evaluating chains of mathematical arguments); modelling skills (e.g., translating "reality" into mathematical structures); problem posing and solving skills; representation skills (e.g., distinguishing between different forms of representation of mathematical situations); symbolic skills; technical skills (e.g., solving equations); communication skills; and skills in using mathematical tools and aids.

[In the OECD/PISA definition of mathematics literacy], the term "engage in mathematics" includes communicating, taking positions towards, relating to, assessing, and even appreciating mathematics (OECD, 1999, p. 41).

Scientific literacy depends on an ability to relate evidence or data to claims or conclusions. In particular, scientific literacy involves the processes of recognising scientifically investigable questions (e.g., identifying the question or idea being tested, distinguishing questions that can be answered by scientific investigation from those which cannot); identifying evidence needed in a scientific investigation (e.g., identifying and recognising what things should be compared, what variables should be changed or controlled, and what additional information is required); drawing or evaluating conclusions (e.g., producing a conclusion from a given set of evidence or data, and identifying assumptions made in reaching a conclusion); and communicating valid conclusions (e.g., producing an argument based on a situation or on data given, expressed in a manner that is appropriate and clear to the intended audience).

The American Association for the Advancement of Science uses the term "scientific habits of mind" in describing processes associated with the application of scientific, mathematical and technological knowledge to everyday life. Individuals who have developed these habits of mind should be able to:

(…) use the habits of mind and knowledge of science, mathematics and technology they have acquired to think about and make sense of many of the ideas, claims, and events that they encounter in everyday life. Accordingly, science literacy enhances the ability of a person to observe events perceptively, reflect on them thoughtfully, and comprehend explanations offered for them. In addition, these internal perceptions and reflections can provide the person with a basis for making decisions and taking action (American Association for the Advancement of Science, 1993, p. 322).

Scientific literacy also includes an understanding of the methods by which science derives evidence to support claims for scientific knowledge, and of the strengths and limitations of science in the real world:

An appreciation of what science is and isn't, of what it can be and cannot be, or of what scientists may or may not claim for science, is surely an essential element of literacy (Zen, 1992, p. 19).

Another important element of literacy (reading, mathematical and scientific) in PISA is the ability to stand apart from arguments, evidence or text, to reflect on these, and to evaluate and criticise claims made. These skills go beyond analysis, problem solving and communication to evaluation and critical reflection.

In the domain of reading literacy,

(…) reflecting on the content of a text requires that the reader connects information found in a text to knowledge from other sources. Readers must also assess the claims made in the text against their own knowledge of the world (…). Readers must be able to develop an understanding of what is said and

intended in a text, and must test that mental representation against what they know and believe on the basis of either prior information, or information found in other texts. Readers must call on supporting evidence from within the text and contrast that with other sources of information, using both general and specific knowledge, and the ability to reason abstractly (OECD, 1999, p. 32).

In the domain of scientific literacy,

An important life skill (…) is the capacity to draw appropriate and guarded conclusions from evidence and information (…), to criticise claims made by others on the basis of the evidence put forward, and to distinguish opinion from evidence-based statements. Science has a particular part to play here since it is concerned with rationality in testing ideas and theories against evidence from the world around (OECD, 1999, p. 59).

A brief summary of some of the processes included in the OECD/PISA definitions of reading literacy, mathematical literacy and scientific literacy is shown in Box 3.

BOX 3. OECD/PISA LITERACY PROCESSES

Reading literacy

"Performing different kinds of reading tasks, such as forming a broad general understanding retrieving specific information, developing an interpretation or reflecting on the content or form of the text."

Mathematical literacy

"Mathematical competencies, e.g., modelling, problem solving; divided into three classes: i) carrying out procedures; ii) making connection and integration for problem solving; and iii) mathematisation, mathematical thinking and generalisation."

Scientific literacy

"Process skills, e.g., recognising scientifically investigable questions, identifying evidence, drawing, evaluating and communicating conclusions, and demonstrating understanding of scientific concepts. These do not depend on a pre-set body of scientific knowledge, but cannot be applied in the absence of scientific content."

Knowledge and understanding

Literacy requires the development of a body of knowledge and understanding. Reading literacy requires a knowledge of words, the ability to decode written text, and a knowledge of grammatical structures. Mathematical literacy requires knowledge of mathematical facts, terms and concepts, and an understanding of mathematical principles. Scientific literacy requires knowledge of scientific facts, terms and concepts, and an understanding of scientific principles and laws.

As individuals' levels of reading literacy, mathematical literacy and scientific literacy develop, they are able to draw on an increasingly rich store of knowledge and an increasingly deep understanding of principles within each domain. The development of knowledge and understanding specific to each domain is an important component of the development of literacy.

But literacy involves much more than the mastery of bodies of knowledge. It also involves an understanding of the methods, processes and limitations of a domain, and the ability to use knowledge, understanding and skills in everyday contexts. For example,

[reading] literacy is not simply reading, but an ability to use print for personal and social ends. It is a functional skill in that it requires the application of various skills in common everyday situations (Venezky et al., 1987, p. 5).

OECD/PISA differs from some other assessment programmes in that it is not primarily an assessment of the extent to which students have mastered bodies of knowledge and skills identified in school curricula. It is not an assessment of achievement in school reading, mathematics and science only. PISA recognises the necessity of curriculum-based knowledge and understanding for reading literacy, mathematical literacy and scientific literacy (see Box 4), but tests for these mainly in terms of the acquisition of broad concepts and skills that allow that knowledge to be applied.

BOX 4. OECD/PISA LITERACY CONTENT

Reading literacy

Reading different kinds of text: continuous text classified by type (e.g., description, narration, exposition, argumentation or instruction) and documents, classified by structure (e.g., forms, calls and advertisements, charts and graphs or tables).

Mathematical literacy

Mathematical content: primarily mathematical "big ideas". In the first cycle, these are change and growth, and space and shape. In future cycles, chance, quantitative reasoning, uncertainty and dependency relationships will also be used.

Scientific literacy

Scientific concepts: e.g., structure and properties of matter, chemical and physical changes, energy transformations, forces and movement, form and function, human biology, biodiversity or genetic control, chosen from the major fields of physics, biology, chemistry, etc., and applied in matters to do with science in life and health, science in Earth and environment, and science in technology.

Context of application

Finally, "literacy" incorporates an awareness and appreciation of the contexts in which texts are constructed, mathematics is used, and science operates, and an ability to apply the knowledge, understanding and skills specific to the appropriate domain to a wide range of contexts in the world outside the classroom. This definition of literacy goes beyond the narrower conceptions of literacy of the 1970s (sometimes called "functional" or "survival" literacy). The focus of these earlier approaches was on minimal skills required to function in adult society.

Reading literacy as it is defined today includes an understanding of the contexts in which written texts are created, and the ability to use this contextual understanding to interpret and reason about texts. Modern definitions also recognise that reading literacy plays a crucial role in facilitating participation in a wide variety of social contexts. In the OECD/PISA definition,

> *"participate" includes social, cultural and political engagement. Participation may include a critical stance, a step towards personal liberation, emancipation and empowerment. The term "society" includes economic and political as well as social and cultural life (OECD, 1999, p. 21).*

Modern definitions of mathematical and scientific literacy similarly emphasise the importance of recognising and understanding the contexts in which mathematics and science operate and the forces that shape these fields of human activity:

> *To ensure the scientific literacy of all students, curricula must present the scientific endeavour as a social enterprise that strongly influences – and is influenced by – human thought and action (American Association for the Advancement of Science, 1989, p. 5).*

> *[Being literate] means having the intellectual skills to examine the pros and cons of any technological development, to examine its potential benefits, and to perceive the underlying political and social forces driving the development (Fleming, 1989).*

Beyond an understanding of the contexts in which written texts occur and mathematics and science are undertaken, and the way in which these interact with, influence, and are shaped by context, "literacy" includes an ability to use knowledge, understanding and skills in the three domains in varied contexts and for a range of purposes:

> *[Mathematical literacy] involves using mathematics to make sense of the world; to assist in dealing with real situations which arise in the workplace, personal and community settings. While it necessarily involves understanding mathematical ideas, notations and techniques, it also involves drawing on knowledge of particular contexts and circumstances in deciding when to use mathematics, choosing the mathematics to use, and critically evaluating its use (Cumming, 1997, p. 7).*

In OECD/PISA, reading literacy, mathematical literacy and scientific literacy are assumed to include the ability to apply processes and to use knowledge across a range of contexts:

- Reading literacy includes an ability to read a range of classroom materials and reading materials outside classrooms, including reading for personal use (personal letters, fiction, biography, etc.); public use (official documents, public information, etc.); employment; and education (textbooks, etc.).

- Mathematical literacy includes an ability to apply mathematical knowledge, skills and understandings in "authentic" contexts. A context is considered authentic if it resides in the actual experiences and practices of the participants in a real-world setting. An important part of the definition of mathematical literacy is doing and using mathematics in a variety of situations. These situations include personal life, school life, work and sports (or leisure in general), local community and society as encountered in daily life, and scientific contexts.

- Scientific literacy includes an ability to solve problems in real-world situations which can affect us as individuals (e.g., food and energy use) or as members of a local community (e.g., treatment of the water supply or siting of a power station) or as world citizens (e.g., global warming, diminution of biodiversity). Contexts to which scientific literacy could be applied include self and family (personal), community (public), life across the world (global), and the evolution of scientific knowledge and its influence on social decisions (historical relevance).

Box 5 summarises some of these contexts.

BOX 5. OECD/PISA CONTEXTS OF LITERACY

Reading literacy

"Reading texts written for different situations, e.g., for personal interest or to meet work requirements."

Mathematical literacy

"Using mathematics in different situations, e.g., problems that affect individuals, communities or the whole world."

Scientific literacy

"Using science in different situations, e.g., problems that affect individuals, communities or the whole world."

PISA: a work in progress

The assessment being carried out in 2000 and illustrated in this publication represents the fruition of a long collaborative process. PISA is a highly ambitious venture. Its aim is to make an authentic assessment of how well students are equipped for the future, in a way that is valid across many different cultures and languages. It has brought together scientific expertise from a wide range of participating countries, and has worked in association with governments to produce a survey that will be relevant for policy making. While the first survey will inevitably be able to fulfil some PISA objectives better than others, the achievement so far has been to produce a robust framework that can be developed further over the years.

1

READING LITERACY

ASSESSING READING LITERACY IN PISA

The PISA definition of reading literacy and its context

Reading literacy is defined in PISA as:

> *understanding, using, and reflecting on written texts, in order to achieve one's goals, to develop one's knowledge and potential, and to participate in society.*

Definitions of reading and of reading literacy have changed over time in parallel with social, economic and cultural changes. Literacy is no longer considered simply the ability to read and write. It is viewed as an advancing set of knowledge, skills, and strategies, which individuals build on throughout life.

The PISA definition therefore goes beyond the notion that reading literacy means decoding written material and literal comprehension. Reading incorporates understanding and reflecting on texts. Literacy involves the ability of individuals to use written information to fulfil their goals, and of complex modern societies to use written information to function effectively. PISA 2000 employs some 140 reading literacy items that aim to represent the kinds of literacy that 15-year-olds will face in their future lives.

Three dimensions of reading literacy

Readers respond to a given text in a variety of ways as they seek to use and understand what they are reading. This dynamic process has many dimensions, three of which are used to construct the PISA assessment:

- **"Process" – reading tasks**: various tasks required of readers (such as retrieval of information or interpretation of text) used in PISA to simulate the types of task that students will encounter in real life;

- **Content – types of text**: the form in which written material is encountered and needs to be understood (many and varied forms such as narrative prose, or graphic presentation), a wide selection of which is represented in the PISA assessment items;

- **Context – purpose of text**: the situation in which reading takes place (*e.g.* for private or occupational use), defined in PISA according to how the author intended the text to be used. PISA items are designed to relate to a variety of such contexts.

Reading tasks

PISA assesses students' ability to perform a variety of reading tasks. It aims to simulate the kinds of task encountered in "authentic" reading situations — i.e. in real life. To this end, the assessment measures five aspects of understanding a text. It is expected that all readers, irrespective of their overall proficiency, will be able to demonstrate some level of competency in each aspect. While there is an interrelationship among the five aspects, since each may require many of the same underlying skills, successfully accomplishing one may not be dependent upon successfully completing any other. The five aspects of reading assessed in PISA are:

1. Forming a broad general understanding

This requires the reader to consider the text as a whole or in a broad perspective. Students may be asked, for example, to demonstrate initial understanding by identifying the main

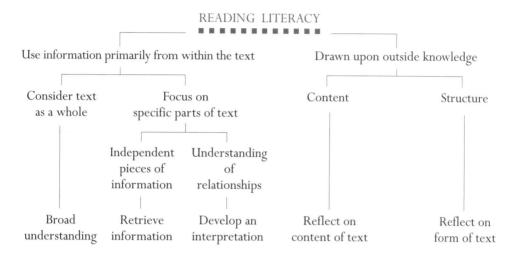

READING LITERACY

Use information primarily from within the text — Drawn upon outside knowledge

Consider text as a whole — Focus on specific parts of text — Content — Structure

Independent pieces of information — Understanding of relationships

Broad understanding — Retrieve information — Develop an interpretation — Reflect on content of text — Reflect on form of text

topic of the text, to explain the purpose of a map or graph, to match a piece of text to a question about the broad purpose of the text, or to focus on more than one specific reference in the text and to deduce the theme from the repetition of a particular category of information. Selecting the main idea implies establishing a hierarchy among ideas and choosing the most general and overarching ones. Such a task indicates whether the student can distinguish between key ideas and minor details, or can recognise the summary of the main theme in a sentence or title.

2. Retrieving information

In the course of daily life, readers often need a particular piece of information. They may need to look up a telephone number. They may want to check the departure time for a bus or train. They may want to find a particular fact to support or refute a claim someone has made. To retrieve effectively, readers must scan, search, locate, and select relevant information. In assessment tasks that call for retrieving information, students have to identify the essential elements of a message: characters, time, setting, etc. They must match information given in the question with either literal or synonymous information in the text and use this to find

the new information asked for. This may require discriminating between two similar pieces of information. By systematically varying the elements that contribute to difficulty, measurement of various levels of proficient performance associated with this aspect of comprehension can be achieved.

3. Developing an interpretation

This requires readers to extend their initial impressions, processing information in a logical manner so that they develop a more specific or complete understanding of what they have read. Tasks that might be used to assess this aspect include comparing and contrasting information – by integrating two or more pieces of information from the text, drawing inferences about the relationship between different sources of information, and identifying and listing supporting evidence in order to infer the author's intent.

4. Reflecting on the content of a text

This requires the reader to relate information found in a text to knowledge from other sources. Readers must assess the claims made in the text against their own knowledge of the world or against information found in other texts in the assessment or explicitly provided in the question. In many situations, readers must know how to justify their own point of view. Typical assessment tasks include providing evidence or arguments from outside the text, assessing the relevance of particular pieces of information or evidence, drawing comparisons with moral or aesthetic rules (standards), identifying information that might strengthen the author's argument, and evaluating the sufficiency of the evidence or information provided in the text.

5. Reflecting on the form of a text

Tasks in this category require readers to stand apart from the text, consider it objectively, and evaluate its quality and appropriateness. Knowledge of such things as text structure, genre and register play an important role in these tasks. Students are required to detect nuances in language – for example, understanding when the choice of an adjective might colour interpretation. Assessment tasks include determining the utility of a particular text for a specified purpose, evaluating an author's use of certain textual features in accomplishing a particular goal, and identifying or commenting on the author's use of style and what the author's purpose and attitude are.

Table 1. **Distribution of reading tasks by aspects of reading literacy**

Aspect	% of PISA reading literacy assessment
Retrieving information	20
Broad understanding	20
Developing an interpretation	30
Reflecting on content	15
Reflecting on form	15
TOTAL	**100**

Table 1 shows the distribution of reading literacy tasks in the PISA 2000 assessment by each of the five aspects defined above. The first three aspects, which look at how well a student can understand and use information within a text, account for 70 per cent of the reading literacy assessment. The remaining tasks require wider reflection.

Types of text

At the heart of the organisation of the PISA reading assessment is a distinction between *continuous* and *non-continuous* texts. Continuous texts are typically composed of sentences that are, in turn, organised into paragraphs. These may be fit into even larger structures such as sections, chapters, and books. Non-continuous texts, or documents as they are known in some approaches, present information in a variety of different ways, such as forms, graphs and maps.

Continuous texts

Continuous text types are all in a standard "prose" form. They are classified according to the author's purpose, with the following five types used in PISA:

1. *Description* refers to properties of objects in space, and typically provides an answer to "what" questions.

2. *Narration* refers to properties of objects in time and typically provides answers to "when", or "in what sequence" questions.

3. *Exposition* presents information as composite concepts or mental constructs, or those elements into which concepts or mental constructs can be analysed. The text provides an explanation of how the component elements interrelate in a meaningful whole and often answers "how" questions.

4. *Argumentation* presents propositions as to the relationship among concepts, or other

propositions. Argument texts often answer "why" questions.

5. *Instruction* (sometimes called *injunction*) provides directions on what to do and includes procedures, rules, regulations and statutes specifying certain behaviours.

Non-continuous texts

Unlike continuous texts, non-continuous ones vary in form, and are thus classified according to their structure rather than the author's purpose. The following six types are used in PISA:

1. *Forms* are structured and formatted texts which request the reader to respond to specific questions in specified ways. Typical examples are tax forms, immigration forms, visa forms, application forms, statistical questionnaires, etc.

2. *Calls and advertisements* are documents designed to invite the reader to do something, *e.g.*, to buy goods or services, attend gatherings or meetings, elect a person to a public office, etc. The purpose of these documents is to persuade the reader. They offer something and request attention and action at the same time. Advertisements, invitations, summonses, warnings and notices are examples of this document format.

3. *Charts and graphs* are iconic representations of data. They are used for the purposes of scientific argumentation, and also in journals and newspapers to display numerical and tabular public information in a visual format.

4. *Diagrams* often accompany technical descriptions (*e.g.*, demonstrating parts of a household appliance), expository texts, and instructive texts (*e.g.*, illustrating how to assemble a household appliance). It is often useful to distinguish procedural (how to) from process (how something works) diagrams.

5. *Tables and matrices.* Tables are row and column matrices. Typically, all the entries in each column and each row share properties, and thus the column and row labels are part of the information structure of the text. Common tables include timetables, spreadsheets, order forms and indexes.

6. *Maps* are non-continuous texts that indicate the geographic relationships between places. There is a variety of types of maps. Road maps mark the distances and routes between identified places. Thematic maps indicate the relationships between locations and social or physical features.

Table 2

Distribution of reading tasks by types of text

Text type	% of PISA reading literacy assessment
Narative	13
Expository	22
Descriptive	13
Argumentative / Persuasive	13
Injunctive	5
TOTAL CONTINOUS TEXTS	**66**
Charts / Graphs	11
Tables	11
Diagrams	3
Maps	3
Forms	3
Advertisements	2
TOTAL NON-CONTINOUS TEXTS	**33**

The distribution and variety of texts that students are asked to read for PISA, shown in Table 2, is an important characteristic of the assessment. Continuous texts represent about two-thirds of the texts contained in the assessment, of which the largest single category is expository materials. Two-thirds of non-continuous texts are tables or charts and graphs. The remaining non-continuous texts are maps, advertisements, and forms of the type that 15-year-olds are expected to be able to read and use.

Purposes of text

PISA distinguishes four types of reading situation: reading for private use, reading for public use, reading for work, and reading for education.

While it is the intent of the PISA reading literacy assessment to measure the kinds of reading that occur both within and outside classrooms, the manner in which reading situations are defined cannot be based simply on where reading takes place. For example, textbooks are read both in schools and in homes, and the processes and purposes of reading these texts differ little from one setting to another.

In PISA, the reading situations can therefore be understood as a general categorisation of texts based on their intended use, on implicit or explicit relations to others, and on the general contents. Close attention has therefore been paid to the origin and content of texts. The goal is to reach a balance between reflecting the broad definition of reading literacy used in PISA and representing the linguistic and cultural diversity of participating countries. This diversity will help to ensure that no one group is either advantaged or disadvantaged by the assessment content.

1. *Reading for private use* (personal) is carried out to satisfy an individual's own interests, both practical and intellectual. It also includes reading to maintain, or develop, personal connections to other people. Contents typically include personal letters, fiction, biography, and informational texts read for curiosity, as a part of leisure or recreational activities.

2. *Reading for public use* is carried out to participate in the activities of the larger society. It includes the use of official documents as well as information about public events. In general, these tasks are associated with more or less anonymous contact with others.

3. *Reading for work* (occupational) may not yet be required by most 15-year-olds, but there are two important reasons to include such situations in PISA. First, reading in such situations is usually closely associated with the accomplishment of some immediate task. Secondly, some reading abilities will help to equip students for the world of work into which the PISA target population will shortly move.

4. *Reading for education*, or reading to learn, is normally involved with acquiring information as part of a larger learning task. The materials are often not chosen by the reader, but assigned by a teacher. The content is usually designed specifically for the purpose of instruction.

Table 3 shows the distribution of reading literacy tasks in the assessment across all four situations. The occupational situation is given less weight because of the likelihood that 15-year-olds are relatively unfamiliar with this category of text. It is also important to reduce the potential dependence on specific occupational knowledge that can result when occupational texts are selected.

Table 3
Distribution of reading literacy tasks by purpose of text

Purpose of text	% of PISA reading literacy assessment
Personal	28
Educational	28
Occupational	16
Public	28
TOTAL	**100**

Format of test questions

Just over half of the reading literacy assessment (55 per cent) will be based on multiple-choice items and other questions with more or less specified answers requiring little subjective judgement on the part of the marker. The rest, 45 per cent, will require students to construct their own answers and markers to exercise some judgement in assessing them. This latter category will account for 65 per cent of tasks requiring reflection on content and form, but only 35 per cent of the other three categories of reading task.

Marking

While multiple-choice items have either a right or a wrong answer, partial credit models allow for more complex marking of other items. Psychometric models for such marking are well established and in some ways are preferable to the "right or wrong" approach as they make use of more of the information that is in the answers. Partial credit marking will be used for at least some of the more complex items in which students construct their own answers. It is important to note that markers are advised to ignore spelling and grammar errors, unless they completely obscure the meaning because this assessment is not seen as a test of written expression. The PISA marking scheme for open-ended items is shown at the end of this chapter.

Sample questions

The following examples illustrate the range of tasks and questions used in the PISA assessment of reading literacy. These items were used in the PISA field trial but not selected for the PISA 2000 assessment because of their similarity to other item sets in terms of what they measure. The intention in presenting these tasks and questions is to demonstrate the connection between the PISA assessment framework and the items that have been constructed to represent it.

The results from the field trial is indicative only since they were not based on a probability sample. They are based on a judgement sample drawn from 32 countries which were given equal weight.

Since the PISA 2000 assessment was not completed by the time this publication was produced, items from the PISA 2000 assessment could not be included in this publication for reasons of test security.

Questions use both multiple-choice and open-ended formats. Not all the questions relating to each unit are given here, the aim being to provide a cross-section only. The kinds of continuous texts shown in Unit 1-4 account for about two-thirds of the materials used in the main assessment. Approximately one-third of the texts are non-continuous, exemplified here by Units 5 and 6.

READING UNIT 1
BEES

The following information is from a booklet about bees. Refer to the information to answer the questions below.

COLLECTING NECTAR

Bees make honey to survive. It is their only essential food. If there are 60,000 bees in a hive about one third of them will be involved in gathering nectar which is then made into honey by the house bees. A small number of bees work as foragers or searchers. They find a source of nectar, then return to the hive to tell the other bees where it is.

Foragers let the other bees know where the source of the nectar is by performing a dance which gives information about the direction and the distance the bees will need to fly. During this dance the bee shakes her abdomen from side to side while running in circles in the shape of figure 8. The dance follows the pattern shown on the following diagram.

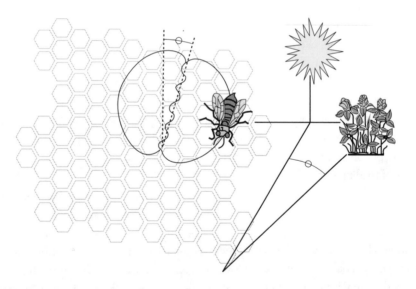

The diagram shows a bee dancing inside the hive on the vertical face of the honeycomb. If the middle part of the figure 8 points straight up it means that bees can find the food if they fly straight towards the sun. If the middle part of the figure 8 points to the right, the food is to the right of the sun.

The distance of the food from the hive is indicated by the length of time that the bee shakes her abdomen. If the food is quite near the bee shakes her abdomen for a short time. If it is a long way away she shakes her abdomen for a long time.

MAKING HONEY

When the bees arrive at the hive carrying nectar they give this to the house bees. The house bees move the nectar around with their mandibles, exposing it to the warm dry air of the hive. When it is first gathered the nectar contains sugar and minerals mixed with about 80% water. After ten to twenty minutes, when much of the excess water has evaporated, the house bees put the nectar in a cell in the honeycomb where evaporation continues. After three days, the honey in the cells contains about 20% water. At this stage, the bees cover the cells with lids which they make out of beeswax.

At any one time the bees in a hive usually gather nectar from the same type of blossom and from the same area. Some of the main sources of nectar are fruit trees, clover and flowering trees.

GLOSSARY

house bee	a worker bee which works inside the hive
mandible	mouth-part

Reproduced from "Hum Sweet Hum".
© National Foundation for Educational Research 1993.

The text in Unit 1 is from an educational context and is an example of a descriptive-explanatory text because it characterises the food-gathering behaviour of bees. It is also an example of a text that contains both continuous and non-continuous information in that it includes a diagram which makes a major contribution to explaining the dance of the forager bees.

Sample Question 1 (Multiple Choice)

• *Aspect*: *Forming a broad understanding*
• *Text type*: *Continuous (description)*
• *Situation*: *Educational*

WHAT IS THE PURPOSE OF THE BEES' DANCE?
A TO CELEBRATE THE SUCCESSFUL PRODUCTION OF HONEY.
B TO INDICATE THE TYPE OF PLANT THE FORAGERS HAVE FOUND.
C TO CELEBRATE THE BIRTH OF A NEW QUEEN BEE.
D TO INDICATE WHERE THE FORAGERS HAVE FOUND FOOD.

Ninety-one per cent of all students participating in the field trial were able to select D as the correct answer to Sample Question 1.

Sample Question 2 (Multiple Choice)

- *Aspect*: *Developing an interpretation*
- *Text type*: *Continuous (description)*
- *Situation*: *Educational*

WHAT IS THE MAIN DIFFERENCE BETWEEN NECTAR AND HONEY?

(A) THE PROPORTION OF WATER IN THE SUBSTANCE.

B THE PROPORTION OF SUGAR TO MINERALS IN THE SUBSTANCE.

C THE TYPE OF PLANT FROM WHICH THE SUBSTANCE IS GATHERED.

D THE TYPE OF BEE WHICH PROCESSES THE SUBSTANCE.

> *Sample Question 2 appears to be slightly more difficult, since only 72 per cent of all students in the PISA field trial answered it correctly. It requires students to develop an interpretation by following the flow of ideas presented in the paragraph under heading "Making Honey."*

Sample Question 3 (Open-Constructed Response)

- *Aspect*: *Developing an interpretation*
- *Text type*: *Continuous (description)*
- *Situation*: *Educational*

IN THE DANCE, WHAT DOES THE BEE DO TO SHOW HOW FAR THE FOOD IS FROM THE HIVE?

> *In Sample Question 3, readers again need to be able to follow the flow of ideas presented in a part of the text. In this case it is the paragraph after the diagram beginning "The distance of the food …". Students were required to state two things: the shaking of the abdomen and the length of time. This question was answered correctly (with full credit) by only 48 per cent of all students. A further 30 per cent responded by stating only one of these facts, and obtained partial credit. The question would have been easier if it had instructed students to list two things stated in the text which bees do in order to indicate how far food is from the hive. Perhaps because of its current wording, only the more careful readers responded with both pieces of information.*

Sample Question 4 (Closed-Constructed Response)

• **Aspect**: *Retrieving information*
• **Text type**: *Continuous (description)*
• **Situation**: *Educational*

WRITE DOWN THREE OF THE MAIN SOURCES OF NECTAR.

1. _____

2. _____

3. _____

In order to respond correctly to Sample Question 4, students need to locate the last sentence in the text that states:"Some of the main sources of nectar are fruit trees, clover and flowering trees." Given that the information is set out in the text and that the question specifically asks for three sources, it is somewhat surprising that only 66 per cent of all students answered correctly. As the question makes no specific reference to the text, it is possible that students attempted to use their own background knowledge to answer this question rather than locating the information stated in the last sentence of the text.

READING UNIT 2

IN POOR TASTE

The following letter appeared in a newspaper in 1997. Refer to the letter to answer the questions below.

IN POOR TASTE
from Arnold Jago

Did you know that in 1996 we spent almost the same amount on chocolate as our government spent on overseas aid to help the poor?

Could there be something wrong with our priorities?

What are you going to do about it?

Yes, you.

Arnold Jago,

Mildura

Source: The Age, 1st April, 1997.

The text shown in Unit 2 is one of the shortest continuous or prose texts in the initial item pool. It is a letter entitled "In Poor Taste" which appeared in a newspaper, and it is classed as an argumentative text because the writer is attempting to persuade the reader of his view. It is drawn from a public context.

Sample Question 5 (Multiple Choice)

• **Aspect**: *Developing an interpretation*
• **Text type**: *Continuous (description)*
• **Situation**: *Public*

ARNOLD JAGO'S AIM IN THE LETTER IS TO PROVOKE

(A) GUILT.

B AMUSEMENT.

C FEAR.

D SATISFACTION.

Sample Question 5 is a multiple-choice question which was answered correctly by, on average, 81 per cent of all students in the countries participating in the PISA field trial. This letter is classified as an argumentative text because the writer was attempting to persuade the reader and it is thought to be a public text since reading it is typically associated with participation in society at large and also because it deals with information involving public events. It is designed to discover whether students can understand the way in which the information in the letter is organised. To this end, students are asked to use the information stated in the letter to make an inference about the author's intent or purpose. They are not asked to judge whether the letter fulfils that intent or purpose (had the question asked the students to consider the utility of the letter in meeting the author's goal or intent, then it would have been classified as reflecting on the form of a text).

Sample Question 6 (Open-Constructed Response)

• **Aspect**: *Reflecting on the content*
• **Text type**: *Continuous (argumentation)*
• **Situation**: *Public*

WHAT KIND OF RESPONSE OR ACTION DO YOU THINK ARNOLD JAGO WOULD LIKE HIS LETTER TO PROMPT?

Sample Question 6 proved more difficult, being correctly answered by only 63 per cent of all students in the PISA field trial. It assesses a different aspect of reading, requiring students to go beyond the information provided in the letter and to reflect on the content. That is, they are not given credit for a correct response if they only state that Jago wants them to spend less on chocolate or to be less greedy. In reflecting on what they read, students need to bring their outside knowledge to bear on their understanding of the letter and to provide a statement or sentence indicating that government or individuals should provide larger amounts of overseas aid or that there should be a shift in priorities.

How did the students answer? Examples (*See end of chapter for marking scheme*)

- "People spending less money on chocolate and more on the overseas sick." (Score 1 [a])

- "That people don't spend all their money on chocolate rather than overseas." (Score 1 [a])

- "An increase in the spending of the government towards overseas aid to help the poor." (Score 1 [a])

- "People instead of buying and eating chocolate should give to a good cause and not be so self-indulgent." (Score 1 [a])

- "People stirred up to think more of helping others than indulging in personal pleasures." (Score 1 [b])

- "People's awareness that the poor need our help, for people to do something about it." (Score 1 [b])

- "I think he would like letters with written opinions and what they should do to help this problem." (Score 0 [e])

- "He may like to see people's suggestions on how to fund raise for overseas using chocolate." (Score 0)

[a], [b] and [e] *refer to the scoring guide at the end of this chapter.*

READING UNIT 3
A JUST JUDGE

Refer to the following story "A Just Judge" to answer the questions below.

A JUST JUDGE

An Algerian king named Bauakas wanted to find out whether or not it was true, as he had been told, that in one of his cities lived a just judge who could instantly discern the truth, and from whom no rogue was ever able to conceal himself. Bauakas exchanged clothes with a merchant and went on horseback to the city where the judge lived.

At the entrance to the city a cripple approached the king and begged alms of him. Bauakas gave him money and was about to continue on his way, but the cripple clung to his clothing.

"What do you wish?" asked the king. "Haven't I given you money?"

"You gave me alms," said the cripple, "now grant me one favour. Let me ride with you as far as the city square, otherwise the horses and camels may trample me."

Bauakas sat the cripple behind him on the horse and took him as far as the city square. There he halted his horse, but the cripple refused to dismount.

"We have arrived at the square, why don't you get off?" asked Bauakas.

"Why should I?" the beggar replied. "This horse belongs to me. If you are unwilling to return it, we shall have to go to court."

Hearing their quarrel, people gathered around them shouting:

"Go to the judge! He will decide between you!"

Bauakas and the cripple went to the judge. There were others in court, and the judge called upon each one in turn. Before he came to Bauakas and the cripple he heard a scholar and a peasant. They had come to court over a woman: the peasant said she was his wife, and the scholar said she was his. The judge heard them both, remained silent for a moment, and then said:

"Leave the woman here with me, and come back tomorrow."

When they had gone, a butcher and an oil merchant came before the judge. The butcher was covered with blood, and the oil merchant with oil. In his hand the butcher held some money, and the oil merchant held onto the butcher's hand.

"I was buying oil from this man," the butcher said, "and when I took out my purse to pay him, he seized me by the hand and tried to take all my money away from me. That is why we have come to you – I holding onto my purse, and he holding onto my hand. But the money is mine, and he is a thief."

Then the oil merchant spoke. "That is not true," he said. "The butcher came to me to buy oil, and after I had poured him a full jug, he asked me to change a gold piece for him. When I took out my money and placed it on a bench, he seized it and tried to run off. I caught him by the hand, as you see, and brought him here to you."

The judge remained silent for a moment, then said: "Leave the money here with me, and come back tomorrow."

When his turn came, Bauakas told what had happened. The judge listened to him, and then asked the beggar to speak.

"All that he said is untrue," said the beggar. "He was sitting on the ground, and as I rode through the city he asked me to let him ride with me. I sat him on my horse and took him where he wanted to go. But when we got there he refused to get off and said that the horse was his, which is not true."

The judge thought for a moment, then said, "Leave the horse here with me, and come back tomorrow."

The following day many people gathered in court to hear the judge's decisions.

First came the scholar and the peasant.

"Take your wife," the judge said to the scholar, "and the peasant shall be given fifty strokes of the lash."

The scholar took his wife, and the peasant was given his punishment.

Then the judge called the butcher.

"The money is yours," he said to him. And pointing to the oil merchant he said: "Give him fifty strokes of the lash."

He next called Bauakas and the cripple.

"Would you be able to recognise your horse among twenty others?" he asked Bauakas.

"I would," he replied.

"And you?" he asked the cripple.

"I would," said the cripple.

"Come with me," the judge said to Bauakas.

They went to the stable. Bauakas instantly pointed out his horse among the twenty others. Then the judge called the cripple to the stable and told him to point out the horse. The cripple recognised the horse and pointed to it. The judge then returned to his seat.

"Take the horse, it is yours," he said to Bauakas. "Give the beggar fifty strokes of the lash."

When the judge left the court and went home, Bauakas followed him.

"What do you want?" asked the judge. "Are you not satisfied with my decision?"

"I am satisfied," said Bauakas. "But I should like to learn how you knew that the woman was the wife of the scholar, that the money belonged to the butcher, and that the horse was mine and not the beggar's."

"This is how I knew about the woman: in the morning I sent for her and said: 'Please fill my inkwell.' She took the inkwell, washed it quickly and deftly, and filled it with ink; therefore it was work she was accustomed to. If she had been the wife of the peasant she would not have known how to do it. This showed me that the scholar was telling the truth.

"And this is how I knew about the money: I put it into a cup full of water, and in the morning I looked to see if any oil had risen to the surface. If the money had belonged to the oil merchant it would have been soiled by his oily hands. There was no oil on the water; therefore, the butcher was telling the truth.

"It was more difficult to find out about the horse. The cripple recognised it among twenty others, even as you did. However, I did not take you both to the stable to see which of you knew the horse, but to see which of you the horse knew. When you approached it, it turned its head and stretched its neck toward you; but when the cripple touched it, it laid back its ears and lifted one hoof. Therefore I knew that you were the horse's real master."

Then Bauakas said to the judge: "I am not a merchant, but King Bauakas, I came here in order to see if what is said of you is true. I see now that you are a wise judge. Ask whatever you wish of me, and you shall have it as reward."

"I need no reward," replied the judge. "I am content that my king has praised me."

Source: "A Just Judge" by Leo Tolstoy from *Fable and Fairytales*, translated by Ann Dunningan.

A third example of a continuous text (Unit 3) is a narrative entitled "A Just Judge". This story depicts a sequence of events beginning with an Algerian king named Bauakas who wants to learn whether it is true that a just judge who is able to discern truth lives in one of his cities. Whereas "In Poor Taste" (Unit 2) is an example of a short text, "A Just Judge" is an example of a long text that students are expected to be able to read and understand. Although 15-year-olds might typically encounter such a text in a classroom, it is classified as a personal rather than educational text, since it is a piece of fiction composed for personal rather than for formal instructional purposes.

Sample Question 7

(Multiple Choice)

• *Aspect*: *Reflecting on the content*
• *Text type*: *Continuous (narration)*
• *Situation*: *Personal / educational*

HOW DID THE JUDGE KNOW THAT THE WOMAN WAS THE WIFE OF THE SCHOLAR?

A BY OBSERVING HER APPEARANCE, AND SEEING THAT SHE DID NOT LOOK LIKE A PEASANT'S WIFE.

B BY THE WAY THE SCHOLAR AND THE PEASANT TOLD THEIR STORIES IN COURT.

C BY THE WAY SHE REACTED TO THE PEASANT AND THE SCHOLAR IN COURT.

D BY TESTING HER SKILL IN WORK THAT SHE NEEDED TO PERFORM FOR HER HUSBAND.

Sample Question 7 is the easiest question associated with this text (answered correctly by 82 per cent of students in the PISA field trial). The correct answer, D, is very similar to the statement in the text, which reads, "...therefore it was work she was accustomed to."

Sample Question 8 (Multiple Choice)

- *Aspect*: Developing an interpretation
- *Text type*: Continuous (narration)
- *Situation*: Personal / educational

WHY DIDN'T BAUAKAS WANT TO BE RECOGNISED?

A HE WANTED TO SEE IF HE WOULD STILL BE OBEYED WHEN HE WAS AN "ORDINARY" PERSON.

B HE PLANNED TO APPEAR IN A CASE BEFORE THE JUDGE, DISGUISED AS A MERCHANT.

C HE ENJOYED DISGUISING HIMSELF SO HE COULD MOVE ABOUT FREELY AND PLAY TRICKS ON HIS SUBJECTS.

(D) HE WANTED TO SEE THE JUDGE AT WORK IN HIS USUAL WAY, UNINFLUENCED BY THE PRESENCE OF THE KING.

In Sample Question 8, which is somewhat more difficult, the text states only that the king exchanged clothes with a merchant and went on horseback to where the judge lived. The reader must infer the motive for this behaviour from the surrounding text. Seventy per cent of the students assessed in the PISA field trial selected alternative D, the correct answer to this question.

Sample Question 9 (Multiple Choice)

- *Aspect*: Forming a broad understanding
- *Text type*: Continuous (narration)
- *Situation*: Personal / educational

WHAT IS THIS STORY MAINLY ABOUT?

A MAJOR CRIMES.

(B) WISE JUSTICE.

C A GOOD RULER.

D A CLEVER TRICK.

Sample Question 9, of similar difficulty to Sample Question 8, asks students to form a broad understanding of the text by identifying the theme or main idea from a list of alternatives. Seventy-two per cent of all students answered it correctly by selecting alternative B.

Sample Question 10 (Multiple Choice)

- **Aspect**: *Reflecting on the form*
- **Text type**: *Continuous (narration)*
- **Situation**: *Personal / educational*

WHICH ONE OF THE FOLLOWING BEST DESCRIBES THE STORY?

(A) A FOLK TALE

B A TRAVEL STORY

C A HISTORICAL ACCOUNT

D A TRAGEDY

E A COMEDY

Sample Question 10, which students in the PISA field trial found more difficult, asks students to show that they understand not only the content of the story but also something about its style and structure. Sixty-four per cent of all students were able to recognise the rhetorical structure of this narrative as a folk tale.

Sample Question 11 (Open-Constructed Response)

- **Aspect**: *Reflecting on the content*
- **Text type**: *Continuous (narration)*
- **Situation**: *Personal / educational*

DO YOU THINK IT WAS FAIR OF THE JUDGE TO GIVE THE SAME PUNISHMENT FOR ALL OF THE CRIMES? EXPLAIN YOUR ANSWER, REFERRING TO SIMILARITIES OR DIFFERENCES BETWEEN THE THREE CRIMES.

A full response to Sample Question 11 requires readers to demonstrate an understanding of the crimes and to support their opinion with some reflective remarks. This calls for more complex reflection on the text and the author's message conveyed by the story. For example, one type of correct answer might be:"In all three crimes one person wanted to cheat another, so it is fair that they were punished in the same way." Another would be: "No, the crimes are not all equal; it is much more serious to want to steal someone's wife than it is to steal their money or their horse."

How did the students answer? Examples *(See end of chapter for marking scheme)*

- "No, some of the crimes were worse than others." (Score 1)

- "Yes, they all lied." (Score 1)

- "I don't think it was fair to have the same punishment because they were all different cases." (Score 0)

- "No, because there were different circumstances involved." (Score 0)

- "Yes, all the three cases had a good and bad person, the so-called baddie should've been punished for doing the wrong thing." (Score 0)

Sample Question 12 (Open-Constructed Response)

- *Aspect*: *Reflecting on the content*
- *Text type*: *Continuous (narration)*
- *Situation*: *Personal / educational*

FOR THIS QUESTION YOU NEED TO COMPARE LAW AND JUSTICE IN YOUR COUNTRY WITH THE LAW AND JUSTICE SHOWN IN THE STORY.

QUESTION 12A:

IN THE STORY CRIMES ARE PUNISHED UNDER THE LAW. WHAT IS ANOTHER WAY IN WHICH LAW AND JUSTICE IN YOUR COUNTRY ARE SIMILAR TO THE KIND OF LAW AND JUSTICE SHOWN IN THIS STORY.

QUESTION 12B:

IN THE STORY THE JUDGE GIVES FIFTY STROKES OF THE LASH FOR ALL THE CRIMES. APART FROM THE KIND OF PUNISHMENT, WHAT IS ONE WAY IN WHICH LAW AND JUSTICE IN YOUR COUNTRY ARE DIFFERENT TO THE KIND OF LAW AND JUSTICE SHOWN IN THIS STORY?

In Sample Question 12, students again need to show that they both understand the story and are able to use their outside knowledge — this time to suggest features that are similar and different in their own legal systems. For example, a correct answer stating a similarity would be: "Both sides are allowed to give their version of the truth." Another might be: "The same punishment is often given out for similar crimes." An incorrect answer might include a vague or inaccurate reference to the story, or be irrelevant. An example would be: "Even important rulers of countries can be brought before a judge or taken to court." The second part of the question, requiring students to reflect on the content by identifying a difference, is marked in the same manner and 33 per cent of the students who answered the question got full credit.

How did the students respond? Examples *(See end of chapter for marking scheme)*

Question 12A:

- "That they were taken to court to discuss the outcome." (Score 1)
- "The justice system in this story has an impartial person to decide the truth, the judge." (Score 1)
- "A jury helps to decide". (Score 0)
- "It was the same." (Score 0)

Question 12B:

- "A board of 12 judges – a jury – is used instead of a single judge." (Score 1)
- "There weren't any lawyers or a jury." (Score 1)
- "We do the judging inside the courtroom." (Score 1)
- "The judges don't use little "tests" like the just judge." (Score 1)
- "Don't wear wigs." (Score 0)

READING UNIT 4

BULLYING

The following article appeared in a Japanese newspaper in 1996. Refer to it to answer the questions below.

PARENTS LACKING AWARENESS OF BULLYING

Only one in three parents polled is aware of bullying involving their children, according to an Education Ministry survey released on Wednesday.

The survey, conducted between December 1994 and January 1995, involved some 19,000 parents, teachers and children at primary, junior and senior high schools where bullying has occurred.

The survey, the first of its kind conducted by the Ministry, covered students from the fourth grade up. According to the survey, 22 per cent of the primary school children polled said they face bullying, compared with 13 per cent of junior high school children and 4 per cent of senior high school students.

On the other hand, some 26 per cent of the primary school children said they have bullied, with the percentage decreasing to 20 per cent for junior high school children and 6 per cent for senior high school students.

Of those who replied that they have been bullies, between 39 and 65 per cent said they also have been bullied.

The survey indicated that 37 per cent of the parents of bullied primary school children were aware of bullying targeted at their children. The figure was 34 per cent for the parents of junior high school children and 18 per cent for those of the senior high school students.

Of the parents aware of the bullying, 14 per cent to 18 per cent said they had been told of bullying by teachers. Only 3 per cent to 4 per cent of the parents learned of the bullying from their children, according to the survey.

The survey also found that 42 per cent of primary school teachers are not aware of bullying aimed at their students. The portion of such teachers was 29 per cent at junior high schools and 69 per cent at senior high schools.

Asked for the reason behind bullying, about 85 per cent of the teachers cited a lack of education at home. Many parents singled out a lack of a sense of justice and compassion among children as the main reason.

An Education Ministry official said the findings suggest that parents and teachers should have closer contact with children to prevent bullying.

School bullying became a major issue in Japan after 13-year-old Kiyoteru Okouchi hanged himself in Nishio, Aichi Prefecture, in the fall of 1994, leaving a note saying that classmates had repeatedly dunked him in a nearby river and extorted money from him.

The bullying-suicide prompted the Education Ministry to issue a report on bullying in March 1995 urging teachers to order bullies not to come to school.

Source: Kyodo, *The Japan Times Ltd.*, Tokyo, May 23 1996.

Unit 4 provides another example of continuous prose texts. It is an article selected from a Japanese newspaper. It too is classified as public context. It is a type of narrative text (a news story) with rhetorical features of expository prose. The author raises a problem and in describing the problem he presents facts and ideas, explains their relationships and relates them to the problem. The repeated mention of the acts of the Ministry of Education provides a frame to the expository part of the article. This is a "news story", which is political-argumentative demonstrating the ministry's responsibility and, indeed, responsible behaviour in finding a solution to the problem. The text form is frequently used in the media and it was, therefore, found relevant to represent the reading domain.

Sample Question 13 (Multiple Choice)

• *Aspect*: Retrieving information
• *Text type*: Continuous (exposition)
• *Situation*: Public

WHAT PERCENTAGE OF TEACHERS AT EACH TYPE OF SCHOOL WAS UNAWARE THAT THEIR STUDENTS WERE BEING BULLIED? CIRCLE THE ALTERNATIVE (A, B, C OR D) WHICH BEST REPRESENTS THIS.

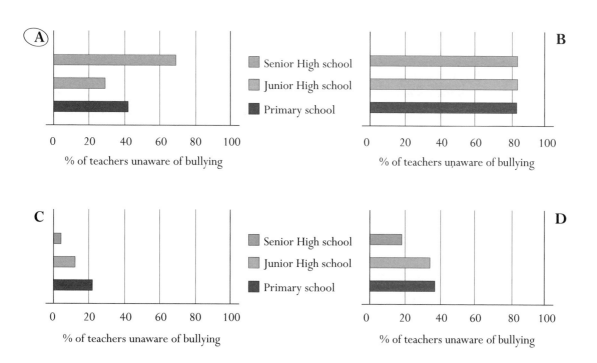

Sample Question 13 requires students to retrieve information that is literally stated in the news article. In order to answer the question correctly, students need to locate the information stated in the paragraph beginning "The survey found that 42 per cent of teachers…" and match it with one of the four alternatives provided in the question. The question was answered correctly by 73 per cent of all students in the PISA field trial. It is made more difficult by the fact that information given in a continuous text has to be matched with a question expressed in graphic, that is, non-continuous form.

Sample Question 14 (Open-Constructed Response)

- *Aspect*: Developing an interpretation
- *Text type*: Continuous (exposition)
- *Situation*: Public

WHY DOES THE ARTICLE MENTION THE DEATH OF KIYOTERU OKOUCHI?

Sample Question 14 appears to be slightly easier (answered correctly by 84 per cent of all students in the PISA field trial). Students are again asked to demonstrate their skill at developing an interpretation. In order to provide a correct answer, students need to be able to link together information contained in the last two paragraphs. They are again asked to demonstrate their skill at interpretation by showing that they can follow the logical organisation and presentation of ideas within a text. It is worth noting that in Sample Question 8 ("A Just Judge"), a multiple-choice format is used to obtain evidence about students' skill at developing an interpretation, while in Sample Question 14 evidence of this skill is gathered through the constructed response format, by asking students to generate a short statement connecting the student's suicide death directly to the increased awareness of bullying and the public's concern for this type of behaviour in Japanese schools.

READING UNIT 5

MORELAND

The Moreland Library System gives new library members a bookmark showing its hours of opening. Refer to the following bookmark to answer the questions below.

Hours of opening – Effective from February 1 1998					
	Brunswick Library	Campbell Turnbull Library	Coburg Library	Fawkner Library	Glenroy Library
Sunday	1pm-5pm	Closed	2pm-5pm	Closed	2pm-5pm
Monday	11am-8pm	11am-5.30pm	1pm-8pm	11am-5.30pm	10am-5.30pm
Tuesday	11am-8pm	11am-8pm	11am-8pm	11am-8pm	10am-8pm
Wednesday	11am-8pm	11am-5pm	10am-8pm	11am-5pm	10am-8pm
Thursday	11am-8pm	11am-5.30pm	10am-8pm	11am-5.30pm	10am-8pm
Friday	11am-5pm	11am-5pm	10am-8pm	11am-5pm	10am-5.30pm
Saturday	10am-1pm	10am-1pm	9am-1pm	10am-1pm	9am-1pm

Sample Question 15

(Closed-Constructed Response)

• **Aspect**: *Retrieving information*
• **Text type**: *Non-continuous (table)*
• **Situation**: *Public*

> *Unit 5 is an example of a non-continuous text. All of the questions associated with this text proved relatively easy, being answered correctly by 91 per cent of all students. Each of the questions is designed to see whether students are able to retrieve information from this type of display.*

AT WHAT TIME DOES THE FAWKNER LIBRARY CLOSE ON WEDNESDAY?

In order to answer Sample Question 15 correctly, students could simply read across the row for Wednesday until they found the hours of operation under the heading Fawkner.

Sample Question 16 (Multiple Choice)

• **Aspect**: *Retrieving information*
• **Text type**: *Non-continuous (table)*
• **Situation**: *Public*

WHICH LIBRARY IS STILL OPEN AT 6 P.M. ON FRIDAY EVENING?

A CAMPBELL TURNBULL LIBRARY

Ⓑ COBURG LIBRARY

C FAWKNER LIBRARY

D GLENROY LIBRARY

E BRUNSWICK LIBRARY

In Sample Question 16, students can again scan across the row labelled "Friday" to determine that only one library stays open past 5:30 p.m.

READING UNIT 6
WARRANTY

Camera Shots **Video House**

89 ELIZABETH STREET, MELBOURNE 3000
PHONE: 9670 9601 FAX: 9602 5527
http://www.camerashots.com.au
CUSTOMER
SARAH BROWN
151 GLENLYON STREET
BRUNSWICK VIC 3057

CAMERA	SHOTS	VIDEO	HOUSE
89			STREET
MELBOURNE	ELIZABETH	VIC	3000
9670 9601			

| INVOICE | 26802 | DATE | 18/10/99 | TIME | 12:10 |
| ACCOUNT | 195927 | SALES | 24 RAY | REG. | 16 |

PRODUCT	DESCRIPTION	SERIAL No	LIST	QTY	NET	TOTAL	EX.
150214	ROLLY FOTONEX 250 ZOOM	30910963		1	249.08	249.08	X
33844	TRIPOD			1	5.66	5.66	X

Transaction . . . . Amount . . . Change
Visa/Bank Card $254.74

Sub-Total	254.74
Total	254.74

Thank you for your business

Above is the receipt that Sarah received when she bought her new camera. Below is the warranty card for the camera. Use these documents to answer the questions which follow.

ONE YEAR WARRANTY: (Private Users)
VALID ONLY IN AUSTRALIA

VIDEO HOUSE & COMPANY PTY LTD – ACN 008 458 884 ('VIDEO HOUSE') warrants to the initial owner that the camera is free of any defects in material or workmanship. This warranty is not transferable.

Video House will service, repair or replace at its election, and free of charge, any part which is found upon inspection by Video House to be defective in material or workmanship during the warranty period(s).

PLEASE PRINT CLEARLY   NO. M 409668

Camera – Model..

....

Serial No: ....

Name of Owner: SARAH BROWN ....

Address: 151 GLENLYON STREET,
          BRUNSWICK VIC 3075

Date Purchased: ....

Purchase Price: ....

[Rubber Stamp of Dealer]

PLEASE NOTE:
Post Immediately – Postage Stamp Necessary
This warranty card should be completed and returned to Video House within 10 days of purchase.
International Warranty Card issued on request.

Another example of a non-continuous text is shown in Unit 6. This text actually consists of two parts: one is the receipt, which contains a variety of information; the other is a warranty card which needs to be completed. Several questions asked about this text provide evidence of students' understanding of, and skill at using, information presented in this format.

Sample Question 17 (Short Response)

- **Aspect**: *Retrieving information*
- **Text type**: *Non-continuous (certificate)*
- **Situation**: *Private*

USE THE DETAILS ON THE RECEIPT TO COMPLETE THE WARRANTY CARD.
THE NAME AND ADDRESS OF THE OWNER HAVE ALREADY BEEN FILLED IN.

Sample Question 17 instructs students to use the information contained in the receipt in order to complete the warranty card. They must retrieve four pieces of information and place them appropriately in the spaces provided. Each piece receives a separate mark, which is combined to yield a single score. Only 44 per cent of students participating in the PISA field trial completed all four parts successfully.

Sample Question 18 (Short Response)

- **Aspect**: *Retrieving information*
- **Text type**: *Non-continuous (certificate)*
- **Situation**: *Private*

HOW LONG DOES SARAH HAVE, TO RETURN THE WARRANTY CARD?

In Sample Question 18, students have to locate the information on the bottom of the warranty card which states that it should be returned within 10 days of purchase. This question was correctly answered by 86 per cent of all students participating in the PISA field trial.

Sample Question 19 (Open-Constructed Response)

- **Aspect**: *Reflecting on content*
- **Text type**: *Non-continuous (certificate)*
- **Situation**: *Private*

THE WORDS "THANK YOU FOR YOUR BUSINESS" ARE PRINTED ON THE BOTTOM OF THE RECEIPT. ONE POSSIBLE REASON FOR THIS IS SIMPLY TO BE POLITE. WHAT IS ANOTHER POSSIBLE REASON?

Sample Question 19 refers to the small print at the bottom of the receipt, but requires an answer which goes beyond the information given in the text. The student must bring his or her outside knowledge to bear on the situation and respond by saying something to the effect that it is there to help promote a positive business-client relationship. This question was answered correctly by only 56 per cent of all students participating in the PISA field trial.

SCORING SCHEME FOR THE READING SAMPLE QUESTIONS

READING UNIT 1 – BEES

Sample Question 1

Score 1: Response option D – To indicate where the foragers have found food.

Score 0: Other.

Sample Question 2

Score 1: Response option A – The proportion of water in the substance.

Score 0: Other.

Sample Question 3

Score 2: Answers which indicate that information is given BOTH by the shaking of the abdomen AND by the length of time for which the abdomen is shaken, for example:

• "How long the bee shakes her abdomen for."

Score 1: Answers which mention the shaking of the abdomen only. (Answer may be partly inaccurate.) For example:

• "She shakes her abdomen."
• "She shows how far it is by how fast she shakes her abdomen."

Score 0: Irrelevant, inaccurate, incomplete or vague answers, for example:

• "How fast the bee runs around in the figure 8."
• "How big the figure 8 is."
• "How the bee moves."
• "The dance."
• "The abdomen."

Sample Question 4

Score 1: (in any order from among the following): abc, abe, bde.

a: fruit trees
b: clover
c: flowering trees
d: trees
e: flowers

Score 0: Other.

READING UNIT 2 – IN POOR TASTE

<u>Sample Question 5</u>

Score 1: Response option A – Guilt.

Score 0: Other.

<u>Sample Question 6</u>

Score 1: Answers of type a or b:

    a. Answers which provide a statement or sentence indicating that government or individuals should spend more on (overseas) aid, for example:
- "People donating money to overseas aid."
- "Donating money to charities."
- "People should spend less on chocolate and more on the poor."

    b. Answers which provide a statement or sentence indicating that government or individuals should change their priorities or awareness, for example:
- "Change our priorities."
- "He would like people to raise their awareness about how we spend our resources."

Score 0: Answers of type c, d or e:

    c. Answers that identify the writer's strategy, to make the reader feel guilty.
- "Feel guilty / ashamed."

    d. Answers which provide a statement or sentence indicating that less should be spent on chocolate or be less greedy, for example:
- "Not buy any more chocolate."
- "Stop eating junk food."

    e. Other, including vague, inappropriate or irrelevant, for example:
- "Spend more on charities."
- "He would like the government to be sacked."
- "He would like people to say, 'I will donate all my money to charity.'"
- "I don't agree with Arnold Jago."
- "Agree with him."

READING UNIT 3 – A JUST JUDGE

<u>Sample Question 7</u>

Score 1: Response option D – By testing her skill in work that she needed to perform for her husband.

Score 0: Other.

<u>Sample Question 8</u>

Score 1: Response option D – He wanted to see the judge at work in his usual way, uninfluenced by the presence of the king.

Score 0: Other.

Sample Question 9

Score 1:   Response option B – Wise justice.

Score 0:   Other.

Sample Question 10

Score 1:   Response option A – A folk tale.

Score 0:   Other.

Sample Question 11

Score 1: Answers of type a:

a. Evaluates the fairness of the punishments in relation to each other, in terms of similarity or difference between offences. Shows accurate understanding of the crimes. For example:
  - "No, it is a much more serious crime to try to steal someone's wife than to steal their money or their horse."
  - "All three criminals tried to cheat someone and then lied about it, so it was fair that they were punished in the same way."
  - "It's hard to say. The peasant, the oil merchant and the beggar all wanted to steal something. On the other hand, the things they wanted to steal were not equally valuable."

Score 0: Other, including answers of type b, c or d:

b. Shows accurate understanding of the crimes and/or the punishments without evaluating them. For example:
  - "The judge gave fifty strokes to the three criminals. Their crimes were stealing a woman, stealing money and stealing a horse."

c. Demonstrates a misunderstanding of the crimes or the punishments. For example:
  - "I think the case of the peasant and the scholar was different from the other two because it was more like a divorce, while the other two were thefts. So the peasant should not have been punished."

d. Agrees or disagrees without explanation or with inadequate explanation. May evaluate the fairness of the punishment per se (*i.e.* answers as if the question were, "Is fifty strokes of the lash a just punishment?"). For example:
  - "No, fifty lashes are much too harsh a punishment for any of these crimes."
  - "Yes, severe punishments are necessary because that way the criminal won't try to do it again."
  - "No, I don't think the punishments were harsh enough."
  - "He was too severe."
  - "Yes, I think it was fair."

Sample Question 12

Question 12A:

Score 1:   Describes one similarity. Shows accurate comprehension of the story. Comparison with a feature of the national legal system is either explicitly stated or may be readily inferred. Accurate knowledge of national legal systems is not essential, but take into account what background knowledge about the law in your country it would be reasonable to expect of a 15-year-old. For example:

- "Rulings are made on evidence."
- "Both sides are allowed to give their version of the truth."
- "Equality before the law (it doesn't matter who you are)."
- "There is a judge presiding over the court."
- "The same punishment is given for similar offences."

Score 0:   Other, including vague, inaccurate and irrelevant answers.

- "Don't know right from wrong."
- "Even important rulers of countries can be called to court."
- "Punishment." [excluded by the question]

Question 12B:

Score 1:   Describes one difference. Shows accurate comprehension of the story. Comparison with a feature of the national legal system is either explicitly stated or may be readily inferred. Accurate knowledge of national legal systems is not essential. (For example "no jury" may be accepted as a "difference", although in some legal systems there is no jury.) Take into account what background knowledge about the law in your country it would be reasonable to expect of a 15-year-old. Examples are:

- "No lawyers."
- "Judge carries out his own investigation."
- "It's very quick, whereas in modern courts usually cases take weeks."
- "No jury; there doesn't seem to be any way of appealing."
- "The punishment is much harsher." [a qualitative comment on the kind of punishment]
- "The same punishment is given regardless of the offence."

Score 0:   Other, including vague, inaccurate and irrelevant answers.

- "Punishment."
- "Old fashioned."
- "Court system."
- "People do not receive the lash." [excluded by question]

READING UNIT 4 – BULLYING

Sample Question 13

Score 1: Response option A – A (letter A or graph A).

Score 0: Other.

Sample Question 14

Score 1:   Answers which relate bullying (and the suicide) to public concern and/or to the survey. The connection may be explicitly stated or readily inferred. Possible answers are:

- "To explain why the survey was conducted."
- "To give the background to why people are so concerned about bullying in Japan."
- "He was a boy who committed suicide because of bullying."
- "To show how far bullying can go."
- "It was an extreme case."

Score 0:   Vague or inaccurate answers:

- "He was a Japanese schoolboy."
- "There are many cases like this all over the world."

READING UNIT 5 – MORELAND

Sample Question 15

Score 1:   5 p.m. *or* 5 o'clock *or* 17.00.

Score 0:   Other.

Sample Question 16

Score 1:   Response option B – Coburg Library.

Score 0:   Other.

READING UNIT 6 – WARRANTY

Sample Question 17

- 1a (model)
    Score 1: Answers which correctly identify the model:
        Rolly Fotonex 250 zoom.
        Rolly Fotonex.
        Fotonex.
    Score 0: Other.

- 1b (serial number)
    Score 1: 30910963.
    Score 0: Other.

- 1c (date of purchase)
    Score 1: 18/10/99.
    Score 0: Other.

• 1d (purchase price)

Score 1:   ($) 249.08.

Score 0:   Other. For example: ($) 254.74.

Sample Question 18

Score 1:   Answers which indicate 10 days *or* ten days. For example:
  • "Within 10 days of purchase."

Score 0:   Other.

Sample Question 19

Score 1:   Answers which refer either explicitly or implicitly to the development of the business-customer relationship. For example:

• "It's good for business to be nice to you."
• "To create a good relationship with the customer."
• "They want you to come back."

Score 0:   Other. For example:

• "They're being polite."
• "They're glad you bought the camera from them."
• "They want you to feel special."
• "To let the customers know they are appreciated."

2

MATHEMATICAL LITERACY

ASSESSING MATHEMATICAL LITERACY IN PISA

The PISA definition of mathematical literacy and its context

Mathematical literacy is defined in PISA as:

> *the capacity to identify, to understand, and to engage in mathematics and make well-founded judgements about the role that mathematics plays, as needed for an individual's current and future private life, occupational life, social life with peers and relatives, and life as a constructive, concerned, and reflective citizen.*

Several aspects of this definition have specific meaning in the PISA context. As with reading, the definition revolves around wider uses in people's lives rather than simply carrying out mechanical operations. The term "literacy" is therefore used to indicate the ability to put mathematical knowledge and skill to functional use rather than just to master it within a school curriculum.

In the PISA definition, to "engage in" mathematics covers not simply physical or social actions (such as working out how much change to give someone in a shop) but also wider uses, including taking positions towards and appreciating things (such as having an opinion about the government's spending plans).

Mathematical literacy also implies the ability to pose and solve mathematical problems in a variety of contexts, as well as the inclination to do so, which often relies on personal traits such as self-confidence and curiosity.

Three dimensions of mathematical literacy

To transform this definition into an assessment of mathematical literacy, three broad dimensions have been identified. These are:

- **Processes**: the focus is on students' abilities to analyse, reason and communicate ideas effectively by posing, formulating and solving mathematical problems. Processes are divided into three classes: reproduction, definitions and computations; connections and integration for problem solving; and mathematisation, mathematical thinking and generalisation.

- **Content**: PISA emphasises broad mathematical themes such as change and growth, space and shape, chance, quantitative reasoning, and uncertainty and dependency relationships.

- **Context**: an important aspect of mathematical literacy is doing and using mathematics in a variety of situations, including personal life, school life, work and sports, local community and society.

Mathematical processes

PISA tasks are designed to encompass a set of general mathematical processes that are meant to be relevant and pertinent to all educational levels:

1. **Mathematical thinking,** which includes:

   - posing questions characteristic of mathematics ("Is there…?", "If so, how many?", "How do we find…?");

   - knowing the kinds of answers that mathematics offers to such questions;

   - distinguishing between different kinds of statements (definitions, theorems, conjectures, hypotheses, examples, conditioned assertions);

– understanding and handling the extent and limits of given mathematical concepts.

2. Mathematical argumentation, which includes:

– knowing what mathematical proof is and how it differs from other kinds of mathematical reasoning;

– following and assessing chains of mathematical arguments of different types;

– possessing a feel for heuristics ("what can(not) happen, and why"), and creating mathematical arguments.

3. Modelling, which includes:

– structuring the field or situation to be modelled;

– mathematising (that is translating from "reality" to "mathematics");

– de-mathematising (that is interpreting mathematical models in terms of "reality");

– tackling the model (working within the mathematics domain);

– validating the model;

– reflecting, analysing, offering a critique of models and their results;

– communicating about the model and its results (including the limitations of such results);

– monitoring and controlling the modelling process.

4. Problem posing and solving, which includes:

– posing and formulating mathematical problems;

– solving different kinds of mathematical problems, in a variety of ways.

5. Representation, which includes:

– decoding, interpreting and distinguishing between different forms of repre-

sentation of mathematical objects and situations, and the interrelations between the various representations;

– choosing, and switching between, different forms of representation, according to situation and purpose.

6. Symbols and formalism, which includes:

– decoding and interpreting symbolic and formal language and understanding its relationship to natural language;

– translating from natural language to symbolic/formal language;

– handling statements and expressions containing symbols and formulae;

– using variables, solving equations and understanding calculations.

7. Communication, which includes:

– expressing oneself, in a variety of ways, on matters with a mathematical component, in oral as well as in written form;

– understanding others' written or oral statements about such matters.

8. Aids and tools, which includes:

– knowing about, and being able to make use of, various aids and tools (including information technology tools) that may assist mathematical activity;

– knowing about the limitations of such aids and tools.

PISA does not use test items that assess the above skills individually. When doing "real mathematics" it is necessary to draw simultaneously upon many of these skills.

In order to describe **levels of mathematical competency,** PISA organises processes into three classes, defining the type of thinking skill needed: i) reproduction, definitions and computations; ii) connections and integration for problem solving; and iii) mathematisation, mathematical thinking, generalisation and insight. In general, these processes are in ascending order of difficulty, but it does not follow that one must be mastered in order to progress to the other: it is possible for example to engage in mathematical thinking without being good at computations.

1. Competency Class 1: Reproduction, definitions and computations

Class 1 covers processes assessed in many standardised tests, as well in comparative international studies, operationalised mainly in multiple-choice format. It deals with knowledge of facts, representing, recognising equivalents, recalling mathematical objects and properties, performing routine procedures, applying standard algorithms and developing technical skills.

2. Competency Class 2: Connections and integration for problem solving

Class 2 processes start making connections between the different strands and domains in mathematics, and integrate information in order to solve simple problems. Although the problems are supposedly non-routine, they require relatively minor degrees of mathematisation.

Within this competency class students are also expected to handle different aspects of representation, according to situation and purpose. Connections also require students to be able to distinguish and relate different statements such as definitions, claims, examples, conditioned assertions and proofs. Decoding and interpreting symbolic and formal language, and understanding its relationship to natural language, form another aspect of this class. In this class, the problems are often placed within a context, and engage students in mathematical decision making.

3. Competency Class 3: Mathematisation, mathematical thinking, generalisation and insight

In this competency class students are asked to mathematise situations: to recognise and extract the mathematics embedded in the situation and use mathematics to solve the problem, analyse, interpret, develop their own models and strategies, and make mathematical arguments, including proofs and generalisations.

These processes involve critical thinking, analysis and reflection. Students should not only be able to solve problems but also to pose problems, to communicate solutions appropriately, and to have insight into the nature of mathematics as a science.

This level, which goes to the heart of mathematics and mathematical literacy, is difficult to test. The multiple-choice format for test items is usually inadequate. Questions with open-ended answers are more suitable, but both the design of such questions and the marking of answers are difficult.

Mathematical content: strands and "big ideas"

School mathematics curricula are usually organised in strands. These strands compartmentalise mathematics and often over-emphasise computation and formulae. At the beginning of the 20th century, mathematics could reasonably be regarded as consisting of some twelve distinct subjects: arithmetic, geometry, algebra, calculus, and so on. Today, however, between sixty and seventy distinct subjects would be a reasonable figure. Some subjects, such as algebra or topology, have split into various sub-fields; others, such as complexity theory or dynamic systems theory, are completely new areas of study. To be relevant, mathematics must reflect the complex patterns in the world around us.

For these and other reasons, PISA took a different approach and organised content around cross-cutting mathematical themes, referred to as "big ideas". For the purpose of PISA, a selection of big ideas has been made that offers sufficient variety and depth to reveal the essentials of mathematics and that relates to the traditional curricular strands. The following list of mathematical big ideas meets this requirement: change and growth; space and shape; quantitative reasoning; uncertainty; and dependency and relationships.

In PISA 2000, the focus is on the first two of these big ideas. They allow a wide range of aspects of the curriculum to be represented, without giving undue weight to number skills.

1. Change and growth

Every natural phenomenon is a manifestation of change. Examples of change include the growth of organisms, the cycle of seasons, the ebb and flow of tides, cycles in unemployment levels and the Dow-Jones index. Some growth processes can be described or modelled by straightforward mathematical functions: linear, exponential, periodic, logistic, either discrete or continuous. But many processes fall into different categories and data analysis is quite often essential. Observing patterns of change in nature and in mathematics is therefore not confined to particular parts of the curriculum such as algebra.

PISA examines students' ability to represent changes in a comprehensible form, to understand the fundamental types of change, to recognise particular types of change when they occur, to apply these techniques to the outside world, and to cope with a changing world to our best advantage.

Many sub-strands of traditional mathematics curricula are involved in tasks of this type. They include, for example, relations, functions and gradients. Considering rates of growth for different growth phenomena leads to linear, exponential, logarithmic, periodic, logistic growth curves and their properties and relations. These, in turn, lead to aspects of number theory. The connections between these ideas and geometrical representations can also play a role.

Growth patterns can be expressed in algebraic forms, which in turn can be represented by graphs. Growth can also be measured empirically, and questions arise as to what inferences can be made from the growth data, how the growth data might be represented, and so on. Data analysis and statistics are relevant curricular strands here.

2. Space and shape

Patterns are encountered everywhere around us: spoken words, music, video, traffic, constructions and art. Shapes are patterns: houses, churches, bridges, starfish, snowflakes, town plans, clover leaves, crystals and shadows.

In understanding space and shape, students need to look for similarities and differences as they analyse the components of form and recognise shapes in different representations and different dimensions. This means that they must be able to understand the relative positions of objects. They must be aware of how we see things and why we see them as we do. They must learn to navigate through space and through constructions and shapes.

Students should therefore be able to understand the relations between shapes and images or visual representations, such as that between a real city and photographs and maps of the same city. They must also understand how three-dimensional objects can be represented in two dimensions, how shadows are formed and must be interpreted, what "perspective" is and how it functions. Described in this way, the study of space and shape is open-ended and dynamic, and fits well both into mathematical literacy and into the mathematical competencies defined for this study.

In PISA 2000, testing time will be evenly distributed between the two big ideas: change and growth and space and shape. In some items at least, marks will not only be awarded for the "correct" answer but also for the different strategies used by students to solve the test items.

Situations and contexts

Students' mathematical insight and understanding need to be assessed in a variety of situations, partly to minimise the chance of students finding that tasks are not culturally relevant.

One can think of a situation as being at a certain distance from the student. The closest is private life (daily life), next is school life, work and sports, followed by the local community and society as encountered in daily life, and furthest away are scientific contexts. In this way one can define a more or less continuous scale of situations.

It is not always clear to what extent the students, performances are affected by their distance from the situations. We cannot say that "closer" contexts are necessarily more attractive

for students, or better suited than more scientific contexts. Indeed, some experts believe that familiarity with the context can be a hindrance, while research suggests that boys do better on experiential knowledge of numbers and measures from the daily world while girls perform better on items where a standard procedure is needed. Secondary school students appear to have less need for a personally relevant context than primary school children.

Whatever the distance from the students, PISA aims to ensure that tasks are based on "authentic" contexts which are likely to occur in a real-world setting. If mathematics education is to prepare students to be active and informed citizens it has to deal with "real" contexts such as pollution problems, traffic safety and population growth. This does not exclude, however, artificial fictional contexts based on the stylised representation of problems – such as a traffic situation in a non-existent town.

Format of test questions and marking

PISA will assess mathematical literacy through a combination of item formats. Some tasks are assessed through multiple-choice questions, typically those associated with simpler mathematical processes.

Open-ended items are preferred for assessing higher-order mathematical processes. Such items often require students to show the steps taken or to explain how the answer was reached. They allow students to demonstrate their level of ability by providing solutions of a range of mathematical complexity. Furthermore, since these responses give valuable information about students' ideas and thinking, which can be fed back into curriculum planning, the marking guides for items included in the main study were designed to include a system of two-digit marking so that the frequency of various types of correct and incorrect response can be recorded. It is important to note that markers are advised to ignore spelling and grammar errors, unless they completely obscure the meaning, because this is not a test of written expression. The PISA marking scheme for open-ended items is shown at the end of this chapter.

Sample questions

The following examples illustrate the range of tasks and questions used in the PISA assessment of mathematical literacy. These items were used in the PISA field trial but not selected for the PISA 2000 assessment because of their similarity to other item sets in terms of what they measure. The intention in presenting these tasks and questions is to demonstrate the connection between the PISA assessment framework and the items that were constructed to represent it.

Since the PISA 2000 assessment was not completed by the time this publication was produced, items from the PISA 2000 tests could not be included in this publication for reasons of test security.

As will be evident from the examples shown here, it is not always easy to match items neatly to the dimensions of mathematics given in the PISA framework. In particular, the three competency classes are not intended to form a strict hierarchy since the competencies used to solve a given problem will vary from student to student. Mathematical problems are also frequently not specific to particular situations.

MATHEMATICS UNIT 1

PIZZAS

A pizzeria serves two round pizzas of the same thickness in different sizes. The smaller one has a diameter of 30 cm and costs 30 zeds. The larger one has a diameter of 40 cm and costs 40 zeds.

© PRIM, Stockholm Institute of Education.

Sample Question 1 (Open-Constructed Response)

- ***Competency class 2*** *: Connections and integration for problem solving*
- ***Big idea****: Change and growth* and/or *Space and shape*
- ***Situation****: Personal*

WHICH PIZZA IS BETTER VALUE FOR MONEY? SHOW YOUR REASONING.

In Unit 1, the stimulus and the question based on it are about the conceptual understanding of the growth rates of areas. A variety of mathematical competencies, of different levels, can be used to solve the problem.

First, students have to identify the relevant mathematics (part of the mathematisation process) as a critical step in the modelling process (which means in this case: 30 cm; 30 zeds; 40 cm; 40 zeds). Students can then solve the problem through qualitative reasoning: as the surface area of a pizza increases faster (quadratic growth) than the price (which appears to be growing linear), the larger pizza is the better deal. This is a very elegant way of solving the problem because the reasoning goes to the kernel of the mathematical argument, and is easily generalisable. Many students will feel more at ease with a quantitative solution, however. They will calculate the area and amount per zed for each of the two pizzas: the area of the smaller pizza per zed is about 24 cm^2, and that of the bigger one 31 cm^2. Other solutions can be expected: for instance students may visualise the problem by drawing the pizzas to scale and to reason from the drawings. If they use graph paper they do not need the formula for the area of a circle, but can still use a "calculation" strategy.

Some students will no doubt answer that the relative prices of the two pizzas are the same. This is a clear misconception.

For most students, this will be a non-routine problem, and connections will be made between different strands and "big ideas": some might even argue that if students use qualitative reasoning, they are employing competencies of Class 3 (mathematical thinking), while most solutions will rely on Class 2 competencies.

MATHEMATICS UNIT 2
COINS

You are asked to design a new set of coins. All coins will be circular and coloured silver, but of different diameters.

Researchers have found out that an ideal coin system meets the following requirements:

• diameters of coins should not be smaller than 15 mm and not be larger than 45 mm.

• given a coin, the diameter of the next coin must be at least 30% larger.

• the minting machinery can only produce coins with diameters of a whole number of millimetres (*e.g.* 17 mm is allowed, 17.3 mm is not).

Sample Question 2 (Open-Constructed Response)

• *Competency class 2*: *Connections and integration for problem solving*
• *Big idea*: *Change and growth*
• *Situation*: *Occupational*

DESIGN A SET OF COINS THAT SATISFY THE ABOVE REQUIREMENTS. YOU SHOULD START WITH A 15 MM COIN AND YOUR SET SHOULD CONTAIN AS MANY COINS AS POSSIBLE.

The problem set in Sample Question 2 shows the constructive and finite use of mathematics. Some degree of modelling and argumentation, and symbolic, formal and technical skills are required, although the calculation skills required are definitely of the lowest level, the problem lying in the complex way in which the information is presented. Mathematisation is called for in order to translate the problem from natural language into more mathematical language.

The format adopted is that of an open-constructed response item as there are ample opportunities for students to adopt different strategies. Many students will start in the order in which the information is given. This means that the first coin has to be 15 mm in diameter. Then they will compute the 30 per cent increase: a mathematically elegant solution would be to state that a 30 per cent increase will lead to exponential growth with a growth factor of 1.3; which leads to the sequence: 15 - 19.5 - 25.35 - 32.955 - 42.8415. This would show a sophisticated level of mathematical understanding, but would still not be correct because of the requirement for whole millimetres. One correct approach is to start with 15, add 30 per cent of 15 and round up to 20 mm before again adding 30 per cent. Continuing this procedure by adding 30 per cent of 20, and so on, the eventual sequence will be 15 - 20 - 26 - 34 - 45. A variety of partially right answers are possible, particularly if students do not read the text carefully enough or do not fully understand the context.

Computational (Class 1) competencies are required, but information must also be integrated so this item has been classified as Class 2. The "big idea" superficially may appear to be space and shape, but this is superficial, since the problem is about percentual or exponential growth within a geometrical context.

MATHEMATICS UNIT 3
LICHEN

A result of global warming is that the ice of some glaciers is melting. Twelve years after the ice disappears, tiny plants, called lichen, start to grow on the rocks.

Each lichen grows approximately in the shape of a circle.

The relationship between the diameter of this circle and the age of the lichen can be approximated with the formula:

$$d = 7.0 \times \sqrt{t-12} \quad \text{for } t \geq 12$$

where d represents the diameter of the lichen in millimetres, and t represents the number of years after the ice has disappeared.

The problem set out in Unit 3 has been modelled already, so that the mathematisation process has been reduced to the matching of the text to the mathematical formula. However, this is not a trivial demand, and calls for symbolic, formal and technical competencies. There is clearly a space and shape component as it involves the growth of circles, but it can be anticipated that the vast majority of students will solve the problem by substituting the values in the formula, almost without realising that they are dealing with shapes. The format of Sample Questions 3 and 4 is clearly that of an open-constructed response item, with limited possibilities for variation in strategy. Although the situation is scientific and hence rather "far away" from the student, the context is only marginally relevant to understanding the problem and finding a solution. Most students will focus on the formula and the necessary substitutions and use the context merely to find out whether it is t or d that they need to substitute.

Sample Question 3 (Open-Constructed Response)

• **Competency class 1**: *Reproduction, definitions, computations*
• **Big idea**: *Change and growth*
• **Situation**: *Scientific*

USING THE FORMULA, CALCULATE THE DIAMETER OF THE LICHEN, 16 YEARS AFTER THE ICE DISAPPEARED.

SHOW YOUR CALCULATION.

In Sample Question 3, students with less than a full understanding of the process will still have a fair chance of finding the correct answer because the question is relatively straightforward. The variation in strategies is very limited, as is the possibility of a partially correct answer. It seems obvious that the first step is to substitute 16 for t in the formula, resulting in the square root of 16 - 12, multiplied by 7. If students have found this they have addressed the essence of the problem, and will be given partial credit. However, they also need to find the correct answer (14) in order to gain full credit. Although the problem does not completely satisfy the "reproduction" criteria that play an important role in Competency Class 1, the substitution required is so fundamental as to form part of the basic tool kit of any student.

How did the students answer? Examples (See end of chapter for marking scheme)

$d = 7.0 \times \sqrt{16 - 12}$ mm

$d = 7.0 \times \sqrt{4}$ mm — Score 2

$d = 14$ mm

$d = 7.0 \times \sqrt{16 - 12}$ mm — Score 1 (Correct substitution but incorrect answer)

$d = 16$ mm

$d = 7.0 \times \sqrt{16 - 12}$ — Score 1 (Incomplete answer)

$d = 7\sqrt{4}$

Sample Question 4 (Open-Constructed Response)

• **Competency class 2**: *Connections and integration for problem solving*
• **Big idea**: *Change and growth*
• **Situation**: *Scientific*

ANN MEASURED THE DIAMETER OF SOME LICHEN AND FOUND IT WAS 35 MILLIMETRES.

HOW MANY YEARS AGO DID THE ICE DISAPPEAR AT THIS SPOT?

SHOW YOUR CALCULATION.

Sample Question 4 is slightly more difficult, because substituting the value of d instead of t causes more computational problems for many students. One may expect trial and error answers. Students may repeat the procedure used in Sample Question 3, guessing at the value of t until they arrive at a reasonable answer. There will again be variations, ranging from a completely correct answer to a correct substitution but incorrect computation, or to trial and error. This may lead to an answer close to the correct one, for instance 36 instead of 37. The question calls for more complex competencies than Sample Question 3.

How did the students answer? Examples *(See end of chapter for marking scheme)*

$$35 = 7.0 \times \sqrt{t - 12}$$
$$5 = \sqrt{t - 12}$$
$$5 = \sqrt{t} - \sqrt{12}$$

— Score 1

Too hard!

$$35 = 7.0 \times \sqrt{t - 12}$$
$$35^2 = 7^2 \times t - 12$$
$$49t = 1\ 237$$
$$t = 25 \text{ years}$$

— Score 1

MATHEMATICS UNIT 4
SHAPES

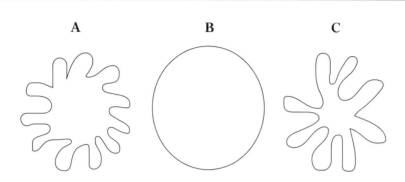

A   **B**   **C**

© PRIM, Stockholm Institute of Education.

Sample Question 5
(Open-Constructed Response)

• **Competency class 1**: *Reproduction, definitions, computations*
• **Big idea**: *Space and shape*
• **Situation**: *Scientific*

Unit 4 clearly relates to familiarity with fundamental ideas about space and shape, including working with measurements. It also depends on the ability to think and work mathematically. The context is at the furthest distance from the student, although it is possible that some students will identify it with some real-life problem within their experience. Sample Questions 5, 6 and 7 are all of the open-constructed response type because a range of strategies can be adopted in order to answer them.

WHICH OF THE FIGURES HAS THE LARGEST AREA? GIVE EXPLANATIONS TO YOUR ANSWER.

Sample Question 5 is relatively simple, calling for competencies of Class 1. It deals with the comparison of three areas, two of them very irregular, and one of them looking like a circle. As each of the two irregular shapes fits more or less into the circle, it may be obvious that the largest area is the "almost circle". This is the "expected" answer, and anything that resembles this line of reasoning will be given full credit. But one still needs to be careful in making judgements: answers are clearly correct if they state that: "B is the largest because it doesn't have indents in it, which decreases the area. A and C have gaps." Or: "B, because it's a full circle, and the others are like circles with bits taken out." An answer could also be expressed in pictures bearing the same message. It is more difficult, however, if a student answers: "B, because it's pretty obvious." Students might indeed find it obvious, but the question clearly states: "Give explanations to your answer." The student in question will not gain full credit.

How did the students answer? *(See end of chapter for marking scheme)*

- "B, because it has no open areas:" (Score 1)

- "B. Because it has the largest surface area." (Score 0)

- "The circle. It's pretty obvious." (Score 0)

- "They are all the same." (Score 0)

Sample Question 6 (Open-Constructed Response)

- ***Competency class 2****: Connections and integration for problem solving*
- ***Big idea****: Space and shape*
- ***Situation****: Scientific*

DESCRIBE A METHOD FOR ESTIMATING THE AREA OF FIGURE C.

Sample Question 6 requires some mathematical reasoning and considerable communication skills. Several approaches are possible. Students might suggest drawing a grid of squares over the shape and counting the squares in a "smart" way. A more sophisticated solution might use realignment in order to get as many squares completely full as possible (by putting poorly filled squares together). Another solution is to cut off the arms and rearrange the pieces so that they fill a square, and then to measure a side of the square. Since experience shows that students are very inventive, one should not be surprised to find solutions that use liquids: "Build a model that uses the shape given as the bottom and build a rim of 1 cm around it. Fill it with water, measure the amount of water and derive the area from that amount."

A separate problem is of technical nature: should the question not be: "Describe a method for estimating the area of figure C in square centimetres"? In order to make an estimation one needs a unit of measure, which is missing in the present problem, and although many students may not see this as an obstacle, it might be wise to specify a unit.

How did the students answer? *(See end of chapter for marking scheme)*

- "You could fill the shape with lots of circles, squares and other basic shapes so there is not a gap. Work out the area of all of the shapes and add together." (Score 1)

- "Redraw the shape onto graph paper and count all of the squares it takes up." (Score 1)

- "Drawing and counting equal size boxes. Smaller boxes = better accuracy." (Score 1 – Here the student's description is brief, but we will be lenient about student's writing skills and regard the method offered by the student as correct).

- "Add up the area of each individual arm of the shape." (Score 0)

- "Find the area of B then find the areas of the cut out pieces and subtract them from the main area." (Score 0)

- "Minus the shape from the circle." (Score 0)

- "Use a string and measure the perimeter of the shape. Stretch the string out to a circle and measure the area of the circle using πr^2." (Score 0 – Here the method described by the student is wrong)

Sample Question 7 (Open-Constructed Response)

- **Competency class 2**: *Connections and integration for problem solving*
- **Big idea**: *Space and shape*
- **Situation**: *Scientific*

DESCRIBE A METHOD FOR ESTIMATING THE PERIMETER OF FIGURE C.

Sample Question 7 is of a similar order of complexity as Sample Question 6, and raises many of the same problems. It tries to establish how well students can measure the perimeter s of an irregular area. A good way is to use measuring tape or a piece of string or cord over the outline of the shape and to measure the length of this string. Students with more developed linear reasoning might suggest approximating the length in straight pieces and subsequently measuring the sum of the pieces. Or students might argue that they could approximate the present irregular star by a regular star shape, and measure the length of one arm, and subsequently multiply the answer by eight.

How did the students answer? Examples *(See end of chapter for marking scheme)*

- "Wool or string!!!" (Score 1 – Here although the answer is brief, the student did offer a METHOD for measuring the perimeter)

- "Cut the side of the shape into sections. Measure each then add them together." (Score 1 – Here the student did not explicitly say that each section needs to be approximately straight, but we will give the benefit of the doubt, that is, by offering the METHOD of cutting the shape into pieces, each piece is assumed to be easily measurable)

- "Measure around the outside." (Score 0 – Here the student did not suggest any METHOD of measuring. Simply saying "measure it" is not offering any method of how to go about measuring it)

- "Stretch out the shape to make it a circle." (Score 0 – Here although a method is offered by the student, the method is wrong)

MATHEMATICS UNIT 5
BRAKING

The approximate distance to stop a moving vehicle is the sum of:

• the distance covered during the time the driver takes to begin to apply the brakes (reaction-time distance)

• the distance travelled while the brakes are applied (braking distance).

The 'snail' diagram below gives the theoretical stopping distance for a vehicle in good braking conditions (a particularly alert driver, brakes and tyres in perfect condition, a dry road with a good surface) and how much the stopping distance depends on speed.

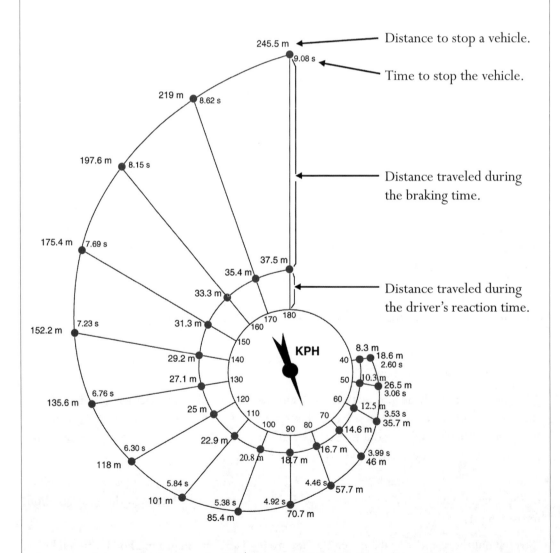

Source: La Prévention Routière, Ministère de l'Éducation nationale, de la Recherche et de la Technologie, France.

Modelling can take many different forms. In Unit 5, a well-known situation that is relevant to everyone who travels by road is presented by way of a diagram to show clearly the increase in braking distance as a function of speed. The context will be familiar for many students. The "distance" from students' own world is relatively small, although they might not be aware of the underlying mathematical model. The context is authentic because it resides in the actual experiences and practices of the participants in a real-life setting. Understanding the problem can certainly contribute to better "functioning" in our complex society, and the ability to interpret and use a visual presentation is a skill that falls well within the limits of literacy. It is not dependent on pure technical skills such as substituting numbers in a known formula.

The modelling of the braking process has already been done, but modelling and representation skills will be used to "de-mathematise" the diagram and translate it into natural language. Basically, all that is asked of the student is to "read" the diagram, making the connection between reaction time, distance and braking action, in relation to speed. This may seem simple but students are so used to seeing in a test what has been taught in the classroom that they lose the ability to transfer their skills to different contexts. The PISA assessment acknowledges this in that all questions are straightforward and use numbers that are directly represented in the diagram. The questions form a natural sequence, using the same speed throughout. It will be clear from the nature of the questions that we do not expect a variety of strategies and styles of answer. The format of Sample Questions 8-12 is therefore that of a closed-con- structed response item. Although this is definitely a simple problem concerning growth curves, it is likely that students will never have encountered such a representation. For that reason all the questions asked about it are assumed to call for Competency Class 2.

The situation (dealing with braking distances diagrammatically) could be used to ask further questions demanding additional skills. If one takes a speed of 107 kph, for instance, the student needs to draw a line (maybe) that starts at the appropriate point on the speedometer between 100 and 110, and then to make educated guesses about the correct answer, which can be obtained in different ways. Much more complex questions could be asked as well. An example would be to compute the ratios between the distances travelled during the reaction time and the total braking distance. At 40 kph this ratio is 8.3:18.6, or close to 1:2. At a speed of 180 kph, the ratio is 37.8:245.5, close to 1:6. Students could be asked to explain that difference.

Sample Question 8 (Closed-Constructed Response)

- **Competency class 2**: *Connections and integration for problem solving*
- **Big idea**: *Change and growth*
- **Situation**: *Personal/public*

IF A VEHICLE IS TRAVELLING AT 110 KPH, WHAT DISTANCE DOES THE VEHICLE TRAVEL DURING THE DRIVER'S REACTION TIME?

For anyone able to read the diagram, the answer to Sample Question 8 is simple: 22.9 m.

Sample Question 9 (Closed-Constructed Response)

- **Competency class 2**: *Connections and integration for problem solving*
- **Big idea**: *Change and growth*
- **Situation**: *Personal/public*

IF A VEHICLE IS TRAVELLING AT 110 KPH, WHAT IS THE TOTAL DISTANCE TRAVELLED BEFORE THE VEHICLE STOPS?

Sample Question 9 is equally simple. The answer is 101 metres.

Sample Question 10 (Closed-Constructed Response)

- **Competency class 2**: *Connections and integration for problem solving*
- **Big idea**: *Change and growth*
- **Situation**: *Personal/public*

IF A VEHICLE IS TRAVELLING AT 110 KPH, HOW LONG DOES IT TAKE TO STOP THE VEHICLE COMPLETELY?

Sample Question 10 is related to the previous question. This question is somewhat less relevant in most cases of braking but can be found at the outer spiral: 5.84 seconds.

Sample Question 11 (Closed-Constructed Response)

- **Competency class 2**: *Connections and integration for problem solving*
- **Big idea**: *Change and growth*
- **Situation**: *Personal/public*

IF A VEHICLE IS TRAVELLING AT 110 KPH, WHAT IS THE DISTANCE TRAVELLED WHILE THE BRAKES ARE BEING APPLIED?

Sample Question 11 is different, requiring not just reading of the diagram but also some simple calculation to show that students can interpret the diagram. Students need to subtract 22.9 from 101 to find the answer, 78.1 metres.

Sample Question 12 (Closed-Constructed Response)

- **Competency class 2**: *Connections and integration for problem solving*
- **Big idea**: *Change and growth*
- **Situation**: *Personal/public*

A SECOND DRIVER, TRAVELLING IN GOOD ROAD CONDITIONS, STOPS HER VEHICLE IN A TOTAL DISTANCE OF 70.7 METRES. AT WHAT SPEED WAS THE VEHICLE TRAVELLING BEFORE THE BRAKES WERE APPLIED?

Sample Question 12, the last on this stimulus, is somewhat easier as it merely requires students to read off the speed that accords with the given total braking distance.

MATHEMATICS UNIT 6
PATIO

Sample Question 13 (Open-Constructed Response)

• *Competency class 2*: *Connections and integration for problem solving*
• *Big idea*: *Space and shape*
• *Situation*: *Personal*

NICK WANTS TO PAVE THE RECTANGULAR PATIO OF HIS NEW HOUSE. THE PATIO IS 5.25 METRES LONG AND 3.00 METRES WIDE. HE NEEDS 81 BRICKS PER SQUARE METRE.

CALCULATE HOW MANY BRICKS NICK NEEDS FOR THE WHOLE PATIO.

An important part of the definition of mathematical literacy is doing and using mathematics in a variety of "authentic" situations. These situations include personal life and work. Unit 6, however simple, fits well into the definition and can be encountered in many variations in daily life or at work.

In order to answer Sample Question 13, the student needs to understand the problem. In this case the wording is straightforward, and confusion is hardly possible. It is almost a "standard" problem: the solution is to compute the total area, and multiply this by the number of bricks needed for one square metre, in this case 81. It could be argued therefore that this problem has two stages. The mathematisation process (finding the relevant mathematics in the text, which is 5.25 times 3.00 and 81 per square metre) is perhaps a third stage. The question itself is a little ambiguous because it uses natural language, asking "how many bricks Nick needs", but this can be translated into at least three possible correct answers. One answer is 1 276. Or one could answer by stating how many "whole" bricks are needed (admittedly somewhat less natural): 1 275. Or one could give a "precise" number of bricks (including partial bricks): 1 275.75. The most likely answer is that 15 square metres takes 1 215 bricks. The three remaining areas are each of 1/4 square metre. Since 1/4 of 81 is about 20, we must add 60 bricks to the total of 1 215, giving 1 275. The format is therefore that of an open-constructed response item, as students have the opportunity to adopt a variety of strategies.

The most obvious competencies required are modelling skill, to mathematise the problem, and problem solving skill to find the correct answer. Communication skill is also needed because there is more than one possible answer, and (as in almost all problems) technical skill is needed for correct computation. Representation skill may be useful if students want to visualise the problem in order to solve it. They might want to draw the patio and divide it up into blocks of 81 bricks. This question seems to fit neatly into Class 2 as it is not a reproduction problem, and requires simple problem solving skills, typical for this level of competencies.

MATHEMATICS UNIT 7

SEALS SLEEP

A seal has to breathe even if it is asleep in the water. Martin observed a seal for one hour. At the start of his observation, the seal was at the surface and took a breath. It then dove to the bottom of the sea and started to sleep. From the bottom it slowly floated to the surface in 8 minutes and took a breath again. In three minutes it was back at the bottom of the sea again. Martin noticed that this whole process was a very regular one.

Sample Question 14 (Multiple Choice)

- **Competency class 2**: *Connections and integration for problem solving*
- **Big idea**: *Change and growth*
- **Situation**: *Personal / Scientific*

AFTER ONE HOUR THE SEAL WAS

A AT THE BOTTOM

B ON ITS WAY UP

C BREATHING

D ON ITS WAY DOWN

Sample Question 14 demonstrates that simple mathematics can be used to make sense of the world around us. Students need to analyse the text carefully and to recognise that the crucial mathematical idea here is periodicity, which falls within the "big idea" of change and growth. They need to transform this idea into a mathematical problem, which can be solved in different ways. This is relatively complex because the information is not neatly organised for students: first, they are given information about the diving part of the cycle, but not about the time it takes. They find this information only after the numerical information about the floating process. This is not what students are usually confronted with. They need to grasp that a full cycle takes 11 minutes: three minutes to dive, eight minutes to float to the surface, take a breath, and dive again. The mathematisation of the problem is that at $t = 0$, the seal starts to dive, at $t = 3$, it is at the bottom, and at $t = 11$ it is at the surface again. And so on. What is it doing at $t = 60$? Answer: if five cycles take 55 minutes, at $t = 60$ we are 5 minutes after the beginning of the cycle, and hence on its way up to the surface. But students could also mathematise the problem by using less formal mathematics. They could make a sketch with the surface and the bottom as two parallel lines and draw lines down (3 mins.) and up (8 mins.), continuing this process until they reach the 60 minute mark. The *competencies used here are modelling, representation and formal skills. Many variations and other strategies can be expected.*

The problem is not "close" to most students' worlds. It is somewhat scientific although students might encounter this or similar problems nearer to home: predicting tides for those close to the sea, or arrival times of regular buses. The problem therefore is authentic, although it has been pre-modelled. The format is multiple choice, and machine marking is possible.

SCORING SCHEME FOR THE MATHEMATICS SAMPLE QUESTIONS

MATHEMATICS UNIT 1 – PIZZA

Sample Question 1

Score 1: Answers which give the general reasoning that the surface area of pizza increases more rapidly than the price of the pizza, concluding that the larger pizza is better value. For example:

- "The diameter of the pizzas is the same number as their price, but the amount of pizza you get is found using squarred diameter, so you will get more pizza per *zeds* from the larger one."

  or

Answers which calculate the area and amount per *zed* for each pizza, concluding that the larger pizza is better value. For example:

- "Area of smaller pizza is 0.25 x π x 30 x 30 = 225π; amount per zed is 23.6 cm^2 area of larger pizza is 0.25 x π x 40 x 40 = 400π; amount per zed is 31.4 cm2 so larger pizza is better value."

Score 0: Other incorrect responses. For example:

- "They are the same value for money."

or

Answers which are correct but with an incorrect or insufficient reasoning. For example:

- "The larger one."

MATHEMATICS UNIT 2 – COINS

Sample Question 2

Score 2: 15 - 20 - 26 - 34 - 45. It is possible that the response could be presented as actual drawings of the coins of the correct diameters. This should be scored 2 as well.

Score 1: The answer gives a set of coins that satisfy the three criteria, but not the set that contains as many coins as possible, for example:

- "15 - 21 - 29 - 39", *or* "15 - 30 - 45."

or

Answers which give the first four diameters correct, the last one incorrect, for example:

- "15 - 20 - 26 - 34 - ."

or

Answers which give the first three diameters correct, the last two incorrect, for example:

- "15 - 20 - 26 - ."

Score 0: Other incorrect responses.

Sample Question 3

Score 2: 14 mm or 14 (units not required). Score 2 should be given as long as the correct answer is 14 whether solution steps are shown or not.

$$d = 7.0 \times \sqrt{16 - 12}$$
$$d = 14$$
⎤ Score 2

• "14 mm."

Score 1: Answers with partial responses, for example:

• Correct substitution of value in the formula but incorrect answer.
• Incomplete answers.

Score 0: Other incorrect responses, for example:

• "16." (Incorrect answer with no solution steps shown).

Sample Question 4

Score 2: Answers which indicate 37 years or 37 (units not required), regardless of the presence or absence of solution steps, for example:

$$35 = 7.0 \times \sqrt{t - 12}$$
$$5 = \sqrt{t - 12}$$
$$25 = t - 12$$
$$t = 37$$
⎤ Score 2

Score 1: Answers which indicate a correct substitution of values in the formula but an incorrect answer, for example:

$$35 = 7.0 \times \sqrt{t - 12}$$
$$35^2 = 7^2 \times t - 12$$
$$35t = 1\ 752$$
$$t = 50$$
⎤ Score 1

$$35 = 7.0 \times \sqrt{t - 12}$$
$$35 = \sqrt{t - 12}$$
$$1\ 225 = t - 12$$
$$t = 1\ 237$$
⎤ Score 1

Score 0: Other incorrect responses.

MATHEMATICS UNIT 4 – SHAPES

Sample Question 5

Score 1: Answers which indicate shape B, supported with plausible reasoning, for example:

• "B. It doesn't have indents in it which decreases the area. A and C have gaps."
• "B, because it's a full circle, and the others are like circles with bits taken out."

Score 0: Answers which indicate shape B, without plausible support.

Sample Question 6

Score 1: Answers which indicate any reasonable method, such as:

• "Draw a grid of squares over the shape and count the squares that are more than half filled by the shape."
• "Cut the arms off the shape and rearrange the pieces so that they fill a square then measure the side of the square."
• "Build a 3D model based on the shape and fill it with water. Measure the amount of water used and the depth of the water in the model. Derive the area from the information."

Score 0: Other incorrect or incomplete answers. For example:

• "The student suggests to find the area of the circle and subtract the area of the cut out pieces. However, the student does not mention about HOW to find out the area of the cut out pieces."

Sample Question 7

Score 1: Answers which indicate any reasonable method, such as:
• "Lay a piece of string over the outline of the shape then measure the length of string used."
• "Cut the shape up into short, nearly straight pieces and join them together in a line, then measure the length of the line."
• "Measure the length of some of the arms to find an average arm length then multiply by 8 (number of arms) x 2."

Score 0: Other incomplete or incorrect responses.

MATHEMATICS UNIT 5 – BRAKING

Sample Question 8

Score 1: 22.9 metres (units not required).

Score 0: Other.

Sample Question 9

Score 1: 101 metres (units not required).

Score 0: Other.

Sample Question 10

Score 1: 5.84 seconds (units not required).

Score 0: Other.

Sample Question 11

Score 1: 78.1 metres (units not required).

Score 0: Other.

Sample Question 12

Score 1: 90 kph (units not required).

Score 0: Other.

MATHEMATICS UNIT 6 – PATIO

Sample Question 13

Score 2: Answers which indicate 1 275 or 1 276 (units not required). For example:
• "5.25 x 3 = 15.75 x 81 = 1 276."

Score 1: Partially correct responses. For example:
• "15.75." (units not required)
• "5.25 x 3 = 15.75
  15.75 x 81 = 9 000"
• "5.25 x 3.0 = 15.75 m^2; so 15.75 x 1 275.75 = 1 376 bricks." (*Here the student got the first part right, but the second part wrong. Give credit for the first part and ignore the second part. So score as 1*)

or

• "1 215 bricks for 5m x 3m." (*This is used for students who are able to calculate the number of bricks for an integer number of square metres, but not for fractions of square metres. See example response.*)

5m				
81	81	81	81	81
81	81	81	81	81
81	81	81	81	81

3m

• "81 x 15 = 1 215; 1 215 + 21 = 1 236."

Score 0: Other responses.

MATHEMATICS UNIT 7 – SEALS SLEEP

Sample Question 14

Score 1: Response option B – On its way up.

Score 0: Other.

3

SCIENTIFIC LITERACY

ASSESSING SCIENTIFIC LITERACY IN PISA

The PISA definition of scientific literacy and its context

Scientific literacy is defined in PISA as:

> *the capacity to use scientific knowledge, to identify questions and to draw evidence-based conclusions in order to understand and help make decisions about the natural world and the changes made to it through human activity.*

An important aspect of scientific literacy is that it is considered a key outcome of education by age 15 for all students, whether or not they continue to learn science thereafter. Scientific thinking is required by citizens, not just scientists. It has been widely accepted in the past that reading and mathematical skills are important for all adults, in many life contexts. The inclusion of scientific literacy as a general competency for life reflects the growing centrality of scientific and technological questions to 21st century life. Note that the definition does not imply that tomorrow's adults need large reservoirs of scientific knowledge, but that the key is to be able to think scientifically about the evidence that they encounter.

Three dimensions of scientific literacy

To transform this definition into an assessment of scientific literacy, three broad dimensions have been identified. These are:

- **Scientific processes or skills**: the mental processes that are involved in addressing a question or issue (such as identifying evidence or explaining conclusions);

- **Concepts and content**: the scientific knowledge and conceptual understanding that are required in using these processes;

- **Context**: situations in which the processes and understanding are applied – such as the personal context of health and nutrition or the global context of climate.

Within each dimension, decisions have been made about which components need to be included – for example, what kinds of scientific process are the most important to master. The intention has been to focus on literacy as a broad competence rather than on the mastery of curriculum content only. The arguments and decisions about these components are briefly set out below.

Scientific processes

PISA emphasises the ability to use scientific knowledge and to know about science. The assessment of such abilities helps us to understand how well science education is preparing future citizens to participate in societies ever more affected by scientific and technological advances. Students should be equipped with understanding of the nature of science, of its procedures, of its strengths and limitations and of the kinds of question that it can, and cannot, answer. Students should also be able to recognise the type of evidence required in a scientific investigation and the extent to which reliable conclusions can be drawn from evidence. It is considered important for students to be able to communicate their understanding and arguments effectively to particular audiences, for otherwise they will have no voice in the matters that are debated in society.

It should be possible for all these abilities to be derived from experiencing science at first hand and from investigations and experiments in school. However, the concern in PISA is not to find out whether students can undertake scientific investigations for themselves, but rather whether their school experiences have culminated in an understanding of scientific processes and the ability to apply scientific concepts that enable them "to make decisions about the natural world and the changes made to it through human activity".

These arguments have led to the identification of the following scientific processes for assessment in PISA:

1. Recognising scientifically investigable questions

This means being able to identify the kinds of question that science can attempt to answer, or the specific question that is, or might be, tested in a particular situation.

It can be assessed, for example, by presenting a situation in which questions could be answered scientifically and asking for these to be identified, or presenting several questions and asking which can be answered by scientific investigation.

2. Identifying evidence needed in a scientific investigation

This process involves identifying or proposing the evidence required to answer the questions posed in a scientific investigation, or the procedures needed to gather that evidence.

It can be assessed, for example, by presenting an investigation and asking students to identify the evidence needed or the action to be taken to obtain valid evidence.

3. Drawing or evaluating conclusions

This process involves relating conclusions to the evidence on which they are based, or should be based.

It can be assessed, for example, by providing students with an account of an investigation and the conclusions drawn from it and asking for an evaluation of these conclusions, or by asking for a conclusion or alternative conclusions to be drawn that are consistent with given evidence.

4. Communicating valid conclusions

The process involved here is that of expressing, in a way that is appropriate to a given audience, the conclusions that can be drawn from available evidence.

It can be assessed, for example, by presenting students with a situation which requires information or evidence from different sources to be brought together to support a given course of action or conclusion. The emphasis here is on the clarity of communication rather than the particular conclusion being communicated, provided that this is consistent with scientific understanding.

5. Demonstrating understanding of scientific concepts

This is the process of showing understanding by being able to apply concepts in situations different from those in which they were learned. It involves not only recalling knowledge but also showing the relevance of that knowledge or using it in making predictions or giving explanations.

It can be assessed, for example, by asking for explanations or predictions about a given situation, phenomenon or event.

It is acknowledged and indeed emphasised that in using all of these processes some scientific knowledge is required. This is most obvious in Process 5, but it applies to Processes 1 to 4 equally, for these cannot be described as "scientific processes" unless they are applied in relation to scientific content.

Scientific concepts

The scientific concepts selected in PISA are expressed as broad integrating ideas that help to explain aspects of our material environment. The PISA framework does not attempt to identify all concepts that would meet this criterion; assessing them comprehensively would be impossible within the constraints of limited test "space". Instead, concepts will be sampled from the following main themes:

1. Structure and properties of matter
2. Atmospheric change
3. Chemical and physical changes
4. Energy transformations
5. Forces and movement
6. Form and function
7. Human biology
8. Physiological change
9. Biodiversity
10. Genetic control
11. Ecosystems
12. The Earth and its place in the universe
13. Geological change

Situations and areas of application

The PISA definition of scientific literacy emphasises the application of processes and concepts in relation to problems and issues in the real world. Students who have acquired some measure of scientific literacy will be able to apply what they have learned in school and non-school situations. A scientific situation is used here to indicate a real-world phenomenon in which science can be applied. Note the distinction between a scientific concept (such as atmospheric change) and an aspect of our world in which it is applied (such as weather or climate).

The areas of application of science have been grouped under three broad headings:

1. Science in life and health,
2. Science in Earth and environment, and
3. Science in technology.

Problems and issues under these headings can affect us as individuals, as members of a local community or as world citizens; often as all three. Moreover, some areas in which science is applied have a long history, illustrating changes in scientific understanding over time and providing opportunities for recognising the application of science in contexts that are no longer familiar today.

The situations that can be used for assessing scientific literacy can thus be characterised both by the broad area of application and by the aspects of our lives in which they are relevant (Table 1).

Format of test questions

The test used to assess scientific literacy is a series of "units", each dealing with a particular problem or issue. Assessment units present students with a real-life situation, taken from an authentic source, and a series of questions about it. Each question requires the use of one or more of the process skills and some scientific knowledge. The presentation of the stimulus material (problem or issue) requires the reading of some text, table or diagrammatic representation. However, since several questions are linked to the same stimulus material in each unit, the overall time spent reading, rather than answering a question, is no greater than in a series of stand-alone items in a conventional test.

In the following examples, only two of the planned items within each unit are presented, in the interests of providing a range of situations. There will, therefore, appear to be a greater reading load for each question than is in fact the case for the actual PISA assessment. The commentary on each question indicates the

Table 1

Situations used for assessing scientific literacy

Relevance	Areas of application		
	Science in life and health	**Science in Earth and environment**	**Science in technology**
Personal, Community, Global, Historical.	Health, disease and nutrition; Maintenance and sustainable use of species; Interdependence of physical and biological systems.	Pollution; Production and loss of soil; Weather and climate.	Biotechnology; Use of materials and waste disposal; Use of energy; Transportation.

process that is required for answering, the scientific knowledge that is called upon and the area of application.

In the case of Process 5, the aim is to assess understanding of a scientific concept through applying it to the situation. For Processes 1 to 4, on the other hand, the scientific knowledge that is required is not intended to constitute a major obstacle to answering: it is ability in the process that is being assessed. For some, this appears to mean that answering the question is a matter of "common sense" rather than scientific understanding. However, common sense of this kind is indeed part of scientific literacy, derived from scientific knowledge which has become internalised and part of rational thinking. We make no apology for this; after all, did not Einstein describe science as nothing more than "a refinement of everyday thinking"?

Marking

About two-thirds of the items used in PISA are in a form that can be unambiguously marked as correct or incorrect. Either they are in a fixed-answer form or they require only a few words to be supplied. Other items will require extended responses and can often be marked as incorrect, partially correct or correct. The marking scheme for these open questions provides not only general guidelines but examples of answers for each response category. Furthermore, since these responses give valuable information about students' ideas and thinking, which can be fed back into curriculum planning, the marking guides for items in the main study were revised to include a system of two-digit marking so that the frequency of various types of correct and incorrect responses can be recorded. It is important to note that markers are advised to ignore spelling and grammar errors, unless they completely obscure the meaning, because this is not a test of written expression. The PISA marking scheme for open-ended items is shown at the end of this chapter.

Sample questions

The following examples illustrate the range of tasks and questions used in the PISA assessment of scientific literacy. These items were used in the PISA field trial but not selected for the PISA 2000 assessment because of their similarity to other item sets in terms of what they measure. The intention in presenting these tasks and questions is to demonstrate the connection between the PISA assessment framework and the items that have been constructed to represent it.

Since the PISA 2000 assessment was not completed by the time this publication was produced, items from the PISA 2000 tests could not be included in this publication for reasons of test security.

SCIENCE UNIT 1

BUSES

A bus is moving along a straight stretch of road. The bus driver, named Ray, has a cup of water resting in a holder on the dashboard:

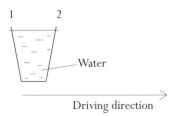

Suddenly Ray has to slam on the brakes.

Sample Question 1 (Multiple Choice)

- **Process**: *Demonstrating understanding of scientific concepts*
- **Concept**: *Forces and movement*
- **Situation / Area of application**: *Science in technology (transportation)*

WHAT IS MOST LIKELY TO HAPPEN TO THE WATER IN THE CUP IMMEDIATELY AFTER RAY SLAMS ON THE BRAKES?

A THE WATER WILL STAY HORIZONTAL.

B THE WATER WILL SPILL OVER SIDE 1.

Ⓒ THE WATER WILL SPILL OVER SIDE 2.

D THE WATER WILL SPILL BUT YOU CANNOT TELL IF IT WILL SPILL OVER SIDE 1 OR SIDE 2.

Sample Question 1 is the first question in a unit about buses, requiring students to consider scientific aspects of a commonly experienced form of transport. The question uses this situation to assess knowledge of the momentum of moving objects and of forces needed to stop movement. When the bus stops quickly, the water in the cup continues to move in the direction in which it is already moving and so is likely to spill over the side furthest forward. The force of reaction against the side of the cup will push the water back, giving rise to the familiar experience in this situation of a liquid spilling both forward and back. However, to identify which side it spills over first requires knowledge of the forces acting on it. The fixed answer form of response is appropriate here since the options are limited.

Sample Question 2 (Open-Constructed Response)

• **Process**: *Drawing or evaluating conclusions*
• **Concept**: *Energy transformations*
• **Situation/Area of application**: *Science in Earth and environment (pollution)*

RAY'S BUS IS, LIKE MOST BUSES, POWERED BY A DIESEL ENGINE. THESE BUSES CONTRIBUTE TO ENVIRONMENTAL POLLUTION.

A COLLEAGUE OF RAY WORKS IN A CITY WHERE THEY USE TROLLEY BUSES. THEY ARE POWERED BY AN ELECTRIC ENGINE. THE VOLTAGE NEEDED FOR SUCH AN ELECTRIC ENGINE IS PROVIDED BY OVERHEAD LINES (LIKE ELECTRIC TRAINS). THE ELECTRICITY IS SUPPLIED BY A POWER STATION USING COAL.

SUPPORTERS OF THE USE OF TROLLEY BUSES IN THE CITY SAY THAT THESE BUSES DON'T CONTRIBUTE TO AIR POLLUTION.

ARE THESE SUPPORTERS RIGHT? EXPLAIN YOUR ANSWER.

Sample Question 2 moves the focus to a different feature of buses, as contributors to air pollution. Atmospheric pollution is a major concern for the future, and it is important that students are able to make informed decisions in relation to it. The introductory text to this question presents a conclusion, drawn by some people, that electrically driven trolley buses do not contribute to air pollution. Students are required to evaluate the validity of this conclusion, using the information given in the question and their own knowledge of the products of burning coal in power stations. To gain credit, students must mention in their answer the pollution caused by the coal-burning power stations that produce the electricity, even if they recognise that the electricity users do not themselves cause pollution.

How did the students answer? Examples *(See end of chapter for marking scheme)*

- "Yes and no. The buses don't pollute the city which is good, but the power station does pollute and that's not very good." (Score 1)

- "The buses do contribute to the air pollution by using fossil fuels but they're not as harmful as normal buses with all their gases." (Score 1)

- "Well they have no outlet so no harmful smoke goes into the air which can damage the Ozone layer, and having electricity created by fossil fuels is also more environmental friendly." (Score 0)

- "Yes, they are. Because electricity isn't harmful for the environment we only use up our Earth's gas." (Score 0)

- "I think these supporters are right as diesel engined buses create more pollution than trolley buses using electricity." (Score 0)

- "Yes, because while burning coal no pollution gases will be set free." (Score 0)

S
c
i
e
n
t
i
f
i
c

L
i
t
e
r
a
c
y

SCIENCE UNIT 2
FLIES

Read the following information and answer the questions below.

A farmer was working with dairy cattle at an agricultural experiment station. The population of flies in the barn where the cattle lived was so large that the animals' health was affected. So the farmer sprayed the barn and the cattle with a solution of insecticide A. The insecticide killed nearly all the flies. Some time later, however, the number of flies was again large. The farmer again sprayed with the insecticide. The result was similar to that of the first spraying. Most, but not all, of the flies were killed. Again, within a short time the population of flies increased, and they were again sprayed with the insecticide. This sequence of events was repeated five times: then it became apparent that insecticide A was becoming less and less effective in killing the flies.

The farmer noted that one large batch of the insecticide solution had been made and used in all the sprayings. Therefore he suggested the possibility that the insecticide solution decomposed with age.

Source: *Teaching About Evolution and the Nature of Science*, National Academy Press, Washington, DC, 1998, p. 75.

The subject of Unit 2, the use of insecticides in agriculture, is one that is gaining in importance. Intensive food production has brought with it greater use of insecticides and herbicides, whose effect we now know tends to diminish with continued use. However, in specific cases, as in that presented in this unit, there could be other reasons besides the development of resistance in the organisms targeted. Thus students are presented here with questions set in a context that involves genuine and important issues.

Sample Question 3
(Open-Constructed Response)

• *Process*: Identifying evidence needed in a scientific investigation
• *Concept*: Chemical and physical changes
• *Situation / Area of application*: Science in life and health (health, disease and nutrition)

THE FARMER'S SUGGESTION IS THAT THE INSECTICIDE DECOMPOSED WITH AGE. BRIEFLY EXPLAIN HOW THIS SUGGESTION COULD BE TESTED.

In Sample Question 3, attention is directed to the farmer's own suggestion for the decline in the effectiveness of insecticide A. Students are asked to identify the kind of evidence that would enable the suggestion to be tested. Scientific knowledge of the meaning of decomposition and of how this would change the chemical make-up, and thus the effect, of insecticide A is a necessary background for understanding this question. There are several scientifically valid ways of finding out whether change in the insecticide was responsible for its reduced effect. One is an experimental approach, involving comparison of new and old batches in a controlled test. Variables which would need to be controlled in this test are the type of fly, age of insecticide and the amount of exposure to insecticide. However, answers of this kind are accepted without explicit reference to these controls, since they are often clearly implied. Partial credit is given for answers which suggest some procedure that is relevant but is not sufficient to make the comparisons necessary.

How did the students answer? Examples *(See end of chapter for marking scheme)*

- "Some flies could be taken. If they would both be put in a separate box you could use a new spray and an older spray and see what the results are." (Score 2)

- "Make one big batch of spray. Have two groups of flies and spray each group every six months. Spray group 1 with the big batch, and group 2 a new batch each time." (Score 2)

- "Try a new bottle of it, then wait till it gets a bit older and the flies come back and then try again." (Score 2)

- "Take batches of the insecticide to a laboratory every few months and have its strength tested." (Score 2)

- "Do the same thing but buy new insecticide each time, hence proving if his theory is right or wrong." (Score 1)

- "Maybe if he sent a fresh batch of the poison to the lab with a batch of the old stuff and get them retested the results may prove his theory." (Score 1)

- "He could test it every year to see if it is not old and would still work." (Score 0)

- "Get a fly from his shed and another shed and spray them each with the insecticide." (Score 0)

Sample Question 4 (Open-Constructed Response)

- **Process**: *Drawing or evaluating conclusions*
- **Concept**: *Physiological change*
- **Situation / Area of application**: *Science in life and health (health, disease and nutrition)*

THE FARMER'S SUGGESTION IS THAT THE INSECTICIDE DECOMPOSED WITH AGE. GIVE TWO ALTERNATIVE EXPLANATIONS AS TO WHY "INSECTICIDE A WAS BECOMING LESS AND LESS EFFECTIVE ..."

EXPLANATION 1:

EXPLANATION 2:

The stimulus for this unit presents observations from which alternative conclusions can be drawn. Sample Question 4 focuses on possible reasons for the diminishing effect of the insecticide, apart from the one suggested by the farmer. In the case of answers referring to the resistance of the flies, scientific knowledge of physiological change and of the possibility of consequent inherited resistance is required. Almost all students assessed in the PISA field trial included this as one of their answers. For example: "With the repeated use of the same insecticide the flies were becoming immune to the formula." The other two accepted explanations involve recognising the possibility of changes in the environmental conditions and a change in the way the insecticide was applied – conclusions which can be drawn from the evidence available. Questions such as this, where there are three (and in some cases, more) possible correct answers but where only two are required, raise a general issue about marking. It can sometimes be argued that one particular answer is worth more than others, and therefore that full credit should be given only when this one is included. In the case of Sample Question 4, the response referring to the acquired resistance of the flies might be considered more important than the other two responses. However, if the question does not signal to the student the preference for one type of answer, it is only fair to treat all responses equally.

How did the students answer? Examples *(See end of chapter for marking scheme)*

- Explanation 1: "With the repeated use of the same insecticide the flies were becoming immune to the formula."
  Explanation 2: "Over time chemicals in the insecticide rose to the top of spray can leaving water diluted (ineffective) at the bottom." (Score 2)

- Explanation 1: "The flies were becoming immune to the spray."
  Explanation 2: "Heat may make it decompose and temperature change." (Score 2)

- Explanation 1: "Maybe the flies developed a defense gene so the insecticide would not work."
  Explanation 2: "He (the farmer) used less each time." (Score 2)

- Explanation 1: "The temperature got very hot and affected the insecticide."
  Explanation 2: "The farmer did not spray the insecticide on the flies properly." (Score 2)

- "He might not have sprayed it properly." (Score 1)

- "The flies could have built up an immunity." (Score 1)

- "There were different types of flies each time." (Score 1)

- "The flies could have been breeding." (Score 0)

- "Because every time he sprayed it it became less and less effective." (Score 0)

- "When there is more of it in the can it is stronger." (Score 0)

SCIENCE UNIT 3
BIODIVERSITY

Read the following newspaper article and answer the questions below.

BIODIVERSITY IS THE KEY TO MANAGING ENVIRONMENT

An ecosystem that retains a high biodiversity (that is, a wide variety of living things) is much more likely to adapt to human-caused environment change than is one that has little.

Consider the two food webs shown in the diagram. The arrows point from the organism that gets eaten to the one that eats it. These food webs are highly simplified compared with food webs in real ecosystems, but they still illustrate a key difference between more diverse and less diverse ecosystems.

Food web B represents a situation with very low biodiversity, where at some levels the food path involves only a single type of organism. Food web A represents a more diverse ecosystem with, as a result, many more alternative feeding pathways.

Generally, loss of biodiversity should be regarded seriously, not only because the organisms that have become extinct represent a big loss for both ethical and utilitarian (useful benefit) reasons, but also because the organisms that remain have become more vulnerable (exposed) to extinction in the future.

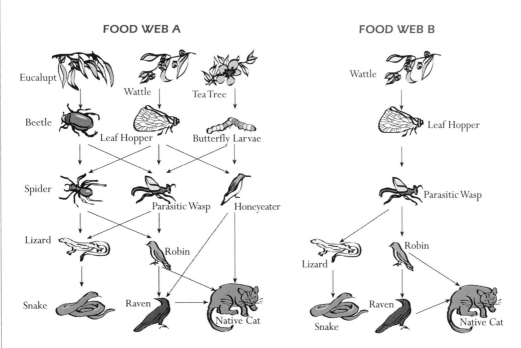

Source: Adapted from Steve Malcolm: "Biodiversity is the key to managing environment", *The Age*, 16 August 1994.

The maintenance of a wide variety of species has far-reaching consequences on a global scale and over a fairly long time span, although its importance may not be immediately obvious in everyday life. The impact of the loss of a species, which can happen for any of a number of reasons, including human activity, may be felt in unexpected ways. Understanding the chain of events and consequences depends on knowledge of the interdependence of living things and the ability to use this knowledge to predict how changes in the population of some living things can affect others. Food webs are a useful way of presenting and explaining such relationships and are encountered universally in science curricula. Unit 3 on biodiversity presents two food webs, one representing a more diverse ecosystem than the other.

Sample Question 5 (Multiple Choice)

- **Process**: *Drawing or evaluating conclusions*
- **Concept**: *Ecosystems*
- **Situation / Area of application**: *Science in life and health (maintenance and sustainable us of species)*

IN THE ARTICLE IT IS STATED THAT "FOOD WEB A REPRESENTS A MORE DIVERSE ECOSYSTEM WITH, AS A RESULT, MANY MORE ALTERNATIVE FEEDING PATHWAYS." LOOK AT FOOD WEB A. ONLY TWO ANIMALS IN THIS FOOD WEB HAVE THREE DIRECT (IMMEDIATE) FOOD SOURCES. WHICH TWO ANIMALS ARE THEY?

(A) NATIVE CAT AND PARASITIC WASP.

B NATIVE CAT AND RAVEN.

C PARASITIC WASP AND LEAF HOPPER.

D PARASITIC WASP AND SPIDER.

E NATIVE CAT AND HONEYEATER.

The first items in the unit (of which Sample Question 5 is one) explore students' ability to "read" the food webs and to interpret correctly what they represent. Sample Question 5 requires students to use their knowledge of food webs and the information given in food web A to identify the conclusion that fits the data. The answer is to be found in the information given in food web A, and students do not have to recall knowledge of the particular animals involved.

Sample Question 6 (Multiple Choice)

• **Process**: *Drawing or evaluating conclusions*
• **Concept**: *Ecosystems*
• **Situation / Area of application**: *Science in life and health (maintenance and sustainable us of species)*

FOOD WEBS A AND B ARE IN DIFFERENT LOCATIONS. IMAGINE THAT LEAF HOPPERS DIED OUT IN BOTH LOCATIONS. WHICH ONE OF THESE IS THE BEST PREDICTION AND EXPLANATION FOR THE EFFECT THIS WOULD HAVE ON THE FOOD WEBS?

A THE EFFECT WOULD BE GREATER IN FOOD WEB A BECAUSE THE PARASITIC WASP HAS ONLY ONE FOOD SOURCE IN WEB A.

B THE EFFECT WOULD BE GREATER IN FOOD WEB A BECAUSE THE PARASITIC WASP HAS SEVERAL FOOD SOURCES IN WEB A.

C THE EFFECT WOULD BE GREATER IN FOOD WEB B BECAUSE THE PARASITIC WASP HAS ONLY ONE FOOD SOURCE IN WEB B.

D THE EFFECT WOULD BE GREATER IN FOOD WEB B BECAUSE THE PARASITIC WASP HAS SEVERAL FOOD SOURCES IN WEB B.

Sample Question 6 is one of several in the unit which explore students' understanding of the impact of change on ecosystems. Other questions require students to generate reasons, in the context of the given food webs, why loss of diversity is regarded seriously. Sample Question 6 requires the comparison of the two food webs and recognition of the greater impact of population change on a less diverse ecosystem. A fixed answer format is used, with emphasis on the reason rather than the choice of food web. Credit is only given for the combination of the correct web and relevant reason. The careful reading of the alternative answers given in the question did not appear to be an obstacle in pilot trials, since the question was answered correctly by 60 per cent of the students in the PISA field trial.

SCIENCE UNIT 4
CLIMATE CHANGE

Read the following information and answer the questions below.

WHAT HUMAN ACTIVITIES CONTRIBUTE TO CLIMATE CHANGE?

The burning of coal, oil and natural gas, as well as deforestation and various agricultural and industrial practices, are altering the composition of the atmosphere and contributing to climate change. These human activities have led to increased concentrations of particles and greenhouse gases in the atmosphere.

The relative importance of the main contributors to temperature change is shown in Figure 1.

Figure 1: **Relative importance of the main contributors to changes in the temperature of the atmosphere**

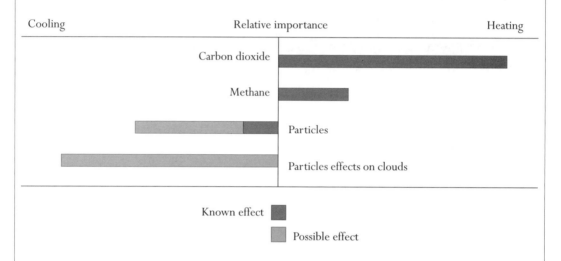

Figure 1 shows that increased concentrations of carbon dioxide and methane have a heating effect. Increased concentrations of particles have a cooling effect in two ways, labelled "Particles" and "Particle effects on clouds".

Bars extending to the right of the centre line indicate a heating effect. Bars extending to the left of the centre line indicate a cooling effect. The relative effect of "Particles" and "Particle effects on clouds" are quite uncertain: in each case the possible effect is somewhere in the range shown by the light grey bar.

Source: Adapted from US Global Change Research Information Office, http://www.gcrio.org/ipcc/qa/04.html

The stimulus material for Unit 4 is taken from information found on the Internet about the contributions of various factors to climate change. The Internet is a source of information that will be used more and more frequently in the lives of today's students. However, some explanation has been added so that the way in which the data is presented presents no obstacle in the task set. The topic is one in which the evidence is inconclusive in relation to possible action that might be taken.

Sample Question 7 (Open-Constructed Response)

• **Process**: *Communicating valid conclusions*
• **Concept**: *Atmospheric change*
• **Situation / Area of application**: *Science in Earth and environment (weather and climate)*

USE THE INFORMATION IN FIGURE 1 TO SUPPORT THE VIEW THAT PRIORITY SHOULD BE GIVEN TO REDUCING THE EMISSION OF CARBON DIOXIDE FROM THE HUMAN ACTIVITIES MENTIONED.

Sample Question 7 requires students to use the information given to support a particular course of action, namely to reduce the emission of carbon dioxide as a result of human activity. A further question (not shown here) asks students to use the same information in a different way, to support the view that the effects of human activity do not constitute a real problem. In both cases, the questions assess the ability to communicate conclusions based on evidence. In combination, the two questions exemplify the caution with which scientific information has to be applied in such complex cases. The questions depend on knowledge of the subject matter, such as why cooling and heating are important in climate change and how carbon dioxide, methane and particles in the air can bring about these effects. However, the focus is on constructing an argument using the given data and thus assesses the ability to communicate effectively. In this example, credit is given for answers which identify the information of relevance to the argument put forward and no credit is given for answers which fail to focus on the argument for reduction, even if they concern the activities that contribute to the production of carbon dioxide.

How did the students answer? Examples *(See end of chapter for marking scheme)*

▪ "The emission of CO_2 causes significant heating to the atmosphere and therefore should be lessened." (Score 1)

▪ "Carbon dioxide in the Earth's atmosphere heats up the Earth. Normally this wouldn't be a problem if the possible effects were proven true. However, they haven't so the graph shows an increase in heat. This shows it is necessary to cut down on carbon dioxide emissions." (Score 1) (*Note*: This answer distinguishes between known and possible effects)

▪ "According to Figure 1 reduction in the emission of carbon dioxide is necessary because it considerably heats the Earth." (Score 1)

▪ "The burning of fossil fuel such as oil, gas and coal are contributing to the build up of gases in the atmosphere, one of which is carbon dioxide (CO_2). This gas affects the temperature of the Earth which increases causing a greenhouse effect." (Score 0)

▪ "The way that humans could help control carbon dioxide levels to drop would be by not driving a car, don't burn coal and don't chop down forests." (Score 0)

SCIENCE UNIT 5

CHOCOLATE

Read the following summary of an article in the newspaper the *Daily Mail* on March 30, 1998 and answer the questions below.

A newspaper article recounted the story of a 22-year-old student, named Jessica, who has a "chocolate diet". She claims to remain healthy, and at a steady weight of 50kg, whilst eating 90 bars of chocolate a week and cutting out all other food, apart from one "proper meal" every five days. A nutrition expert commented: "I am surprised someone can live with a diet like this. Fats give her energy to live but she is not getting a balanced diet. There are some minerals and nutrients in chocolate, but she is not getting enough vitamins. She could encounter serious health problems in later life."

Unit 5 contains several questions bearing on the understanding of a healthy diet and knowledge of the different kinds of food that are needed. The questions lead to the conclusion that the student's chocolate diet is far from healthy and indeed provides more energy than she needs. This unit is presented here to illustrate an engaging and important topic and the variety of questions that can be asked.

In a question not shown here, a further table of information is given from which students have to extract evidence required to test the claim that Jessica's weight remains steady. This question assesses the ability to relate the text to the information given in the table, an aspect of reading literacy. A further question not shown here asks for possible reasons why Jessica may be able to maintain a steady weight despite her excessive intake of energy.

Sample Question 8

(Open-Constructed Response)

- **Process**: *Demonstrating understanding of scientific concepts*
- **Concept**: *Energy transformations*
- **Situation / Area of application**: *Science in life and health (health, disease and nutrition)*

A BOOK WITH NUTRITIONAL VALUES GIVES THE DATA IN TABLE 1 ABOUT CHOCOLATE. ASSUME THAT ALL THESE DATA ARE APPLICABLE TO THE TYPE OF CHOCOLATE JESSICA IS EATING ALL THE TIME. ASSUME ALSO THAT THE BARS OF CHOCOLATE SHE EATS HAVE A WEIGHT OF 100 GRAMS EACH.

Table 1: **Nutritional content of 100 g chocolate**

Proteins	Fats	Carbonhydrates	Minerals		Vitamins			TOTAL ENERGY
			Calcium	Iron	A	B	C	
5 g	32 g	51 g	50 mg	4 mg	-	0.2 mg	-	2 142 kJ

ACCORDING TO THE TABLE, 100 G OF CHOCOLATE CONTAIN 32 G OF FAT AND GIVE 2 142 KJ OF ENERGY. THE NUTRITIONIST SAID: "FATS GIVE HER THE ENERGY TO LIVE.....".

IF SOMEONE EATS 100 G OF CHOCOLATE, DOES ALL THE ENERGY (2 142 KJ) COME FROM THE 32 G OF FAT? EXPLAIN YOUR ANSWER USING DATA FROM THE TABLE.

Sample Question 8 presents information about the nutritional value of chocolate, which is assumed to apply to the type consumed by Jessica. It indicates that chocolate contains some minerals and vitamins as well as fats, protein and carbohydrates. The question posed concerns the energy contributions of these components and requires knowledge that energy comes from fats, proteins and carbohydrates and not from minerals and vitamins, which have other functions in a healthy diet. The question therefore requires not just recall but also application of knowledge in a real-life situation.

Full credit is given for answers which indicate that energy comes not only from the fats but also from the proteins and carbohydrates (one or both) contained in the chocolate. For example: "No, because carbohydrates, for example, provide even more energy than fats." This answer can be regarded as correct because although the amount of energy from 1 g of carbohydrate is smaller than that from 1 g of fat, the student may mean that more carbohydrate is present. Partial credit is given for indicating that energy comes from vitamins and/or minerals as well as proteins and carbohydrates: "I don't think so, because it can also come from the carbohydrates, minerals and vitamins."

Sample Question 9 (Multiple Choice)

• **Process**: *Demonstrating understanding of scientific concepts*
• **Concept**: *Physiological change*
• **Situation/Area of application**: *Science in life and health (health, disease and nutrition)*

THE NUTRITION EXPERTS SAID THAT JESSICA "... IS NOT GETTING NEARLY ENOUGH VITAMINS". ONE OF THOSE VITAMINS MISSING IN CHOCOLATE IS VITAMIN C. PERHAPS SHE COULD COMPENSATE FOR HER SHORTAGE OF VITAMIN C BY INCLUDING A FOOD THAT CONTAINS A HIGH PERCENTAGE OF VITAMIN C IN HER "PROPER MEAL EVERY FIVE DAYS".

HERE IS A LIST OF TYPES OF FOOD.

1.   FISH.
2.   FRUIT.
3.   RICE.
4.   VEGETABLES.

WHICH TWO TYPES OF FOOD FROM THIS LIST WOULD YOU RECOMMEND TO JESSICA IN ORDER TO GIVE HER A CHANCE TO COMPENSATE FOR HER VITAMIN C SHORTAGE?

A   1 AND 2.
B   1 AND 3.
C   1 AND 4.
D   2 AND 3.
E   2 AND 4.
F   3 AND 4.

In Sample Question 9, a correct answer depends on knowledge of the sources of one of the most important components of a healthy diet. This is knowledge that is necessary for students to make informed decisions about their own and others' diets.

SCIENCE UNIT 6
CALF CLONING

Read the following article about the birth of five calves and answer the questions below.

In February 1993 a research team of the National Institute for Agricultural Research in Bresson-Villiers (France) succeeded in producing five clones of calves. The production of the clones (animals with the same genetic material, even though born to five different cows), was a complicated process.

First the researchers removed about thirty egg cells from a cow (let us say the cow's name was Blanche 1). The researchers removed the nucleus from each of the egg cells taken from Blanche 1.

Then the researchers took an embryo from another cow (let us say Blanche 2). This embryo contained about thirty cells.

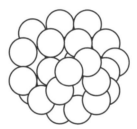

The researchers separated the ball of cells from Blanche 2 into individual cells.

Then they removed the nucleus from each of these individual cells. Each nucleus was injected separately into one of the thirty cells that came from Blanche 1 (cells from which the nuclei had been removed).

Finally the thirty injected egg cells were implanted into thirty surrogate cows. Nine months later, five of the surrogate cows each gave birth to a calf clone.

One of the researchers said that a large scale application of this cloning technique could be financially beneficial for cattle breeders.

Source: Corinne Bensimon, *Libération*, March 1993.

In Unit 6, the text provides an account of an experiment and its outcome. The idea being tested in the experiment is not explicitly stated and students are asked to identify what this could have been.

Sample Question 10 (Open-Constructed Response)

- **Process**: *Recognising scientifically investigable questions*
- **Concept**: *Genetic control*
- **Situation / Area of application**: *Science in technology (biotechnology)*

THE RESULTS OF THE FRENCH EXPERIMENTS ON COWS CONFIRMED THE MAIN IDEA THAT WAS BEING TESTED. WHAT MAIN IDEA COULD HAVE BEEN TESTED IN THIS EXPERIMENT?

A correct answer to Sample Question 10 involves recognising the kind of question that can be addressed in a scientific investigation, in this case in relation to subject matter that requires knowledge of cell division and of the genetic significance of the nucleus of a cell. The marking scheme gives credit for plausible answers, such as "That cloning was possible", which do not mention calves or cows. No credit is given for ideas that could be tested but were not tested in this particular investigation or for ideas that are impossible to answer scientifically.

How did the students answer? *(See end of chapter for marking scheme)*

- That cloning was possible. (Score 1)

- That all cells of cows are the same. (Score 0)

- Mass cloning could be achieved. (Score 0)

Sample Question 11 (Complex Multiple Choice)

- **Process**: *Demonstrating understanding of scientific concepts*
- **Concept**: *Genetic control*
- **Situation / Area of application**: *Science in technology (biotechnology)*

WHICH OF THE FOLLOWING STATEMENTS IS/ARE TRUE? CIRCLE YES OR NO FOR EACH.

STATEMENT:

ALL FIVE CALVES HAVE THE SAME TYPE OF GENES.	YES/NO
ALL FIVE CALVES HAVE THE SAME SEX.	YES/NO
THE HAIR OF ALL FIVE CALVES HAS THE SAME COLOUR.	YES/NO

Here, the question presents statements about the result of cloning in the stimulus article. However, these statements are not drawn from the experimental data and so are not being evaluated in relation to the evidence given. Had this been the case, the process assessed would have been "drawing or evaluating conclusions". Instead, the student has to apply his or her knowledge of genetics in answering. Hence, while the concept and area of application involved are the same as in Sample Question 11, the process is different.

SCORING SCHEME FOR THE SCIENCE SAMPLE QUESTIONS

SCIENCE UNIT 1 – BUSES

Sample Question 1

Score 1:   Response option C – The water will spill over side 2.

Score 0:   Other.

Sample Question 2

Score 1:   Answers which state that the power station or the burning of coal also contributes to air pollution. For example:
• "No, because the power station causes air pollution as well."
• "Yes, but this is only true for the trolley bus itself; burning coal, however, causes air pollution."

Score 0:   No or yes, without a correct explanation.

SCIENCE UNIT 2 – FLIES

Sample Question 3

Score 2: Answers of type a, b or c:

  a. Answers which mention control of all three variables (type of flies, age of insecticide, and exposure), for example:
   • "Compare the results from a new batch of the insecticide with results from the old batch on two groups of flies of the same species that have not been previously exposed to the insecticide."

  b. Answers which mention control of two of the three variables (type of flies, age of insecticide, and exposure), for example:
   • "Compare the results from a new batch of the insecticide with the results from the old batch on the flies in the barn."

  c. Answers which mention control of only one variable of three variables (type of flies, age of insecticide, and exposure), for example:
   • "(Chemically) analyse samples of the insecticide at regular intervals to see if it changes over time."

Score 1: Answers of type d or e:

  d. "Spray the flies with a new batch of insecticide, but without mentioning comparison with old batch."

  e. "(Chemically) analyse samples of the insecticide but without mentioning comparison of analyses over time."
   Note: Score 1 if sending samples of the insecticide to a laboratory is mentioned.

Score 0:   Other.

Sample Question 4

Score 2:   Answers which give any two of the following explanations:

• "Flies with resistance to the insecticide survive and pass on that resistance to later generations (also credit for 'immunity' although it is recognised that it is not strictly analogous to 'resistance')."

• "A change in the environmental conditions (such as temperature)."

• "A change in the way the insecticide was applied (including variation in the amount used)."

Score 1:   Answers which give one explanation from the above.

Score 0:   Other, including new flies moving to the barn from nearby (unsprayed) areas.

SCIENCE UNIT 3 – BIODIVERSITY

Sample Question 5

Score 1:   Response option A – Native Cat and Parasitic Wasp.

Score 0:   Other.

Sample Question 6

Score 1: Response option B – The effect would be greater in food web B because the Parasitic Wasp has only one food source in web B.

Score 0: Other.

SCIENCE UNIT 4 – CLIMATE CHANGE

Sample Question 7

Score 1:   Answers which indicate that:

• Carbon dioxide is relatively the largest contributor to the heating effect and/or the effect of carbon dioxide is a known effect.

or

• Carbon dioxide is relatively the largest contributor to the heating effect and/or the effect of carbon dioxide is a known effect, but which also mention that the possible effects of particles should be considered.

Score 0:   Other, including answers which

• Do not indicate that carbon dioxide is relatively the largest contributor to the heating effect.

or

• Do not focus on the fact that the effects of carbon dioxide are known.

or

• Indicate that an increase in temperature will have a bad effect on the Earth.

or

• Focus on the activities that contribute to carbon dioxide production.

SCIENCE UNIT 5 – CHOCOLATE

Sample Question 8

Score 2:   Answers which indicate "no" and explain that some energy comes from carbohydrates or proteins or carbohydrates + proteins.

Score 1:   Answers which indicate "no" and explain that some energy comes from carbohydrates or proteins or carbohydrates + proteins and also from vitamins and/or minerals.

Score 0:   Answers which
• Indicate "yes".
or
• Indicate "no" with no explanation.
or
• Indicate "no" with irrelevant comment.
or
• Indicate "no" with the explanation that (only) minerals and/or vitamins will contribute to energy as well.
or
• Indicate "no" with the explanation that other components of chocolate (without mentioning them) will contribute as well.

Sample Question 9

Score 1:   Response option E – 2 and 4, alternative E.

Score 0:   Other.

SCIENCE UNIT 6 – CALF CLONING

Sample Question 10

Score 1:   Answers which give an acceptable main idea, for example:
• "Testing whether cloning of calves is possible."
• "Determining the number of calf clones that could be produced."

Score 0:   Answers which
• Do not mention calves or cloning.
or
• In effect repeat that "a large-scale application of this cloning technique could be financially beneficial for cattle breeders".

Sample Question 11

Score 1:   Yes, Yes, Yes.

Score 0:   Other.

REFERENCES

American Association for the Advancement of Science (1989), *Science for all Americans*, New York: Oxford University Press.

American Association for the Advancement of Science (1993), *Benchmarks for Science Literacy*, New York: Oxford University Press.

Applebee, A.N., Langer, J.A. & **Mullis, I.V.S.** (1987), *Learning to be Literate in America: Reading, Writing and Reasoning*, Princeton NJ: Educational Testing Service.

Champagne, A.B. & **Klopfer, L.E.** (1982), "Actions in a time of crisis", *Science Education*, 66(4), pp. 503-514.

Cross, R. (1994), "Scientific literacy and democracy", *Search*, 25(9), pp. 283-286.

Cumming, J. (1997), "Developments in numeracy: what is it and how should we teach it?", *Australian Language Matters*, 5(1), pp. 7-8.

Dangerfield, L. (1989), "Scientific literacy: myth or miracle", *The ACT Science Teacher*, 14(1), pp. 26-31.

Fleming, R. (1989), "Literacy for a technological age", *Science Education*, 73(4), pp. 391-404.

Galbraith, P.L., Carss, M.C., Grice, R.D., Endean, L. & **Warry, M.** (1997), "Towards scientific literacy for the third millenium", *International Journal of Science Education*, 19(4), pp. 447-467.

Kirsch, I.S. & **Murray, T.S.** (1998), *Adult Literacy in OECD Countries: Technical Report on the First International Adult Literacy Survey*, Washington, DC: US Department of Education.

Krugly-Smolska, E.T. (1990), "Scientific literacy in developed and developing countries", *International Journal of Science Education*, 12, pp. 473-480.

OECD (1999), *Measuring Student Knowledge and Skills: A New Framework for Assessment*, Paris: OECD.

Paulos, J.A. (1988), *Innumeracy: Mathematical Illiteracy and its Consequences*, New York: Hill and Wang.

Venezky, R.L., Kaestle, C.F. & **Sum, A.M.** (1987), *The Subtle Danger: Reflections on the Literacy Abilities of America's Young Adults*, Princeton, NJ: Educational Testing Service.

Zen, E. (1992), "Scientific literacy: what it is, why it is important, and what can scientists do to improve the situation?", *The Australian Science Teachers Journal*, 38(3), pp. 18-23.

FURTHER READING

Almond, R.G. & **Mislevy, R.J**. (1998), *Graphical Models and Computerized Adaptive Testing,* TOEFL Technical Report No.14, Educational Testing Service, Princeton, NJ, March.

Baker, L. (1991), "Metacognition, reading and science education", in C. M. Santa and D. E. Alvermann (eds.), *Science Learning: Processes and Applications,* International Reading Association, Newark, DE, pp. 2-13.

Bennett, R.E. (1993), "On the meanings of constructed response", in R.E. Bennett (ed.), *Construction vs. Choice in Cognitive Measurement: Issues in Constructed Response, Performance Testing, and Portfolio Assessment,* Lawrence Erlbaum Associates, Hillsdale, NJ, pp. 1-27.

Binkley, M. & **Linnakylä, P.** (1997), "Teaching reading in the United States and Finland", in M. Binkley, K. Rust and T. Williams (eds.), *Reading Literacy in an International Perspective,* U.S. Department of Education, Washington, DC.

Bruner, J. (1990), *Acts of Meaning,* Harvard University Press, Cambridge, MA.

Bybee, R.W. (1997), "Towards an understanding of scientific literacy", in W. Grabe and C. Bolte (eds.), *Scientific Literacy — An International Symposium,* IPN, Kiel.

Council of Europe (1996), *Modern Languages: Learning, Teaching, Assessment. A Common European Framework of Reference,* CC LANG (95) 5 Rev. IV, Strasbourg.

Council of Ministers of Education, Canada (1994), *Student Achievement Indicators Program: Reading and Writing,* Toronto.

de Lange, J. & **Verhage, H.** (1992), *Data Visualization,* Sunburst, Pleasantville, NY.

de Lange, J. (1987), *Mathematics, Insight and Meaning*, OW and OC, Utrecht.

Devlin, K. (1994, 1997), *Mathematics, The Science of Patterns*, Scientific American Library, New York.

Dole, J., Duffy, G., Roehler, L. & **Pearson, P.** (1991), "Moving from the old to the new: Research on reading comprehension instruction", *Review of Educational Research,* 16 (2), pp. 239-264.

Ehrlich, M.F. (1996), "Metacognitive monitoring in the processing of anaphoric devices in skilled and less-skilled comprehenders", in C. Cornoldi and J. Oakhill (eds.), *Reading Comprehension Difficulties: Processes and Interventions,* Lawrence Erlbaum Associates, Mahwah, NJ, pp. 221-249.

Ehrlich, M. F., Kurtz-Costes, B. & **Loridant, C.** (1993), "Cognitive and motivational determinants of reading comprehension in good and poor readers", *Journal of Reading Behavior, 25,* pp. 365-381.

Einstein, A. (1933), "Preface to M. Plank", *Where is Science Going?,* Allen and Unwin, London.

Elley, W.B. (1992), *How in the World do Students Read?,* International Association for the Evaluation of Educational Achievement, The Hague.

Frederickson, N. (1984), "The real test bias", *American Psychologist, 39,* pp. 193-202.

Freudenthal, H. (1973), *Mathematics as an Educational Task*, Reidel, Dordrecht.

Freudenthal, H. (1983), *Didactical Phenomenology of Mathematical Structures*, Reidel, Dordrecht.

Graeber, W. & **Bolte, C**. (Eds) (1997), *Scientific Literacy – An International Symposium,* IPN, Kiel.

Gronlund, N.E. (1968), *Constructing Achievement Tests*, Prentice Hall, Englewood Cliffs.

Grünbaum, B. (1985), "Geometry strikes again", *Mathematics Magazine*, 58 (1), pp. 12-18.

Hawking, S.W. (1988), *A Brief History of Time,* Bantam Press, London.

Hubbard, R. (1989), "Notes from the underground: Unofficial literacy in one sixth grade", *Anthropology and Education Quarterly, 20,* pp. 291-307.

Jones, S. (1995), "The practice(s) of literacy", in *Literacy, Economy and Society: Results of the First International Adult Literacy Survey,* OECD and Statistics Canada, Paris and Ottawa, pp. 87-113.

Kirsch, I. (1995), "Literacy performance on three scales: Definitions and results", in *Literacy, Economy and Society: Results of the First International Adult Literacy Survey,* OECD and Statistics Canada, Paris and Ottawa, pp. 27-53.

Kirsch, I.S. & **Mosenthal, P.B.** (1989-1991), "Understanding documents. A monthly column", *Journal of Reading,* International Reading Association, Newark, DE.

Kirsch, I. S. & **Mosenthal, P.B.** (1994), "Interpreting the IEA reading literacy scales", in M. Binkley, K. Rust and M. Winglee (eds.), *Methodological Issues in Comparative Educational Studies: The Case of the IEA Reading Literacy Study,* U.S. Department of Education, National Center for Education Statistics, Washington, DC, pp. 135-192.

Kirsch, I., Jungeblut, A. & **Mosenthal, P.B.** (1998), "The measurement of adult literacy", in T. S. Murray, I. S. Kirsch, and L. Jenkins (eds.), *Adult Literacy in OECD Countries: Technical Report on the First International Adult Literacy Survey,* U.S. Department of Education, National Center for Education Statistics, Washington, DC.

Langer, J. (1995), *Envisioning Literature,* International Reading Association, Newark, DE.

Linnakylä, P. (1992), "Recent trends in reading literacy research in Finland", in P. Belanger, C. Winter and A. Sutton (eds.), *Literacy and Basic Education in Europe on the Eve of the 21ˢᵗ Century,* Council of Europe, Strassbourg, pp. 129-135.

Lundberg, I. (1991), "Reading as an individual and social skill", in I. Lundberg and T. Hoien (eds.), *Literacy in a World of Change,* Center for Reading Research/UNESCO, Stavanger.

Maccarthey, S.J. & **Raphael, T.E.** (1989), *Alternative Perspectives of Reading/Writing Connections,* College for Education, Institute for Research on Teaching,. Occasional paper #130, Michigan State University.

Millar, R. & **Osborne, J.** (1998), *Beyond 2000: Science Education for the Future,* King's College London School of Education, London.

Myers, M. & **Paris, S.G.** (1978), "Children's metacognitive knowledge about reading", *Journal of Educational Psychology,* 70, pp. 680-690.

Paris, S., Wasik, B. & **Turner, J.** (1991), "The development of strategic readers", in R. Barr, M. Kamil and P. Mosenthal (eds.), *Handbook of Reading Research,* vol. II, Longman, New York.

Senechal, M. (1990), "Shape", in L.A. Steen (ed.), *On the Shoulders of the Giant — New Approaches to Numeracy,* National Academy Press, Washington D.C., pp. 139-182.

Shamos, M.H. (1995), *The Myth of Scientific Literacy,* Rutgers University Press, New Brunswick.

Smith, M.C. (1996), "Differences in adults' reading practices and literacy proficiencies", *Reading Research Quarterly,* 31, pp. 196-219.

Sticht, T.G. (ed.) (1975), *Reading for Working: A Functional Literacy Anthology,* Human Resources Research Organization, Alexandria, VA.

Stiggins, R.J. (1982), "An analysis of the dimensions of job-related reading", *Reading World,* 82, pp. 237-247.

Streefland, L. (1990), *Fractions in Realistic Mathematics Education, A Paradigm of Developmental Research,* Reidel Dordrecht.

Stuart, I. (1990), "Change", in L.A. Steen (ed.), *On the Shoulders of the Giant — New Approaches to Numeracy,* National Academy Press, Washington D.C., pp. 183-218.

Taube, K. & **Mejding, J.** (1997), "A nine-country study: What were the differences between the low and high performing students in the IEA Reading Literacy Study?", in M. Binkley, K. Rust and T. Williams (eds.), *Reading Literacy in the International Perspectives,* U.S. Department of Education, National Center for Education Statistics, Washington, DC, pp. 63-100.

Traub, R.E. (1993), "On the equivalence of the traits assessed by multiple-choice and constructed-response tests", in R. E. Bennett (ed.), *Construction vs. Choice in Cognitive Measurement: Issues in Constructed Response, Performance Testing, and Portfolio Assessment,* Lawrence Erlbaum Associates, Hillsdale, NJ, pp. 29-44.

Travers, K.J. & **Westbury, I.** (1989), *The IEA Study of Mathematics,* vol. 1, Analysis of mathematics curricula, Pergamon Press, Oxford.

Treffers, A. (1986), *Three Dimensions,* Reidel, Dordrecht.

Treffers, A. & **Goffree, F.** (1985), "Rational analysis of realistic mathematics education", in L. Streefland (ed.), *Proceedings of the Ninth International Conference for the Psychology of Mathematics Education (PME)*, OW and OC, Utrecht, pp. 79-122.

UNESCO (1993*), International Forum on Scientific and Technological Literacy for All,* Final Report, UNESCO, Paris.

Ward, W.C., Dupree, D. & **Carlson, S.B.** (1987), *A Comparison of Free-response and Multiple-choice Questions in the Assessment of Reading Comprehension* (RR-87-20), Educational Testing Service, Princeton, NJ.

Werlich, E. (1976), *A Text Grammar of English,* Quelle and Meyer, Heidelberg.

Ziman, J.M. (1980), *Teaching and Learning about Science and Society,* Cambridge University Press.

APPENDIX 1
FUNCTIONAL EXPERT GROUP MEMBERSHIP

Reading

Irwin Kirsch, Chair
Educational Testing Service
Princeton, New Jersey, United States

Marilyn Binkley
National Center for
Educational Statistics
Washington, DC, United States

Alan Davies
University of Edinburgh, Scotland,
United Kingdom

Stan Jones
Statistics Canada
Nova Scotia, Canada

John de Jong
Swets Language Testing Unit
Arnhem, The Netherlands

Dominique Lafontaine
Université de Liège, Liège,
Belgium

Pirjo Linnakylä
University of Jyvaskyla
Jyvaskyla, Finland

Martine Rémond
Institut National de Recherche
Pédagogique, Paris, France

Wolfgang Schneider
University of Würzburg,
Würzburg, Germany

Ryo Watanabe
National Institute for Educational
Research, Tokyo, Japan

Mathematics

Raimondo Bolletta
Centro Europeo dell'Educazione,
Frascati, Italy

Sean Close
St Patricks College,
Dublin, Ireland

Jan de Lange, Chair
Utrecht University, Utrecht,
The Netherlands

Maria Luisa Moreno
Instituto Nacional de Calidad y
Evaluación (INCE)
Madrid, Spain

Mogens Niss
Roskilde University, Roskilde,
Denmark

Kyung Mee Park
Chungbuk National University,
Seoul, Korea

Thomas Romberg
University of Wisconsin-Madison
Madison, Wisconsin, United States

Peter Schüller
Federal Ministry of Education
and Cultural Affairs
Vienna, Austria

Science

Peter Fensham
Monash University, Melbourne,
Australia

Raul Gagliardi
University of Geneva, Geneva,
Switzerland

Wynne Harlen,
Scottish Council for Research
in Education,
Edinburgh, United Kingdom

Svein Lie
University of Oslo,
Oslo, Norway

Manfred Prenzel
Institut für die Pädagogik der
Naturwissenschaften (IPN)
(Institute for Science Education)
Kiel, Germany

Senta Raizen
National Center for Improving
Science Education
Washington, DC, United States

Donghee Shin
Korea Institute of Curriculum and
Evaluation
Seoul, Korea

Elizabeth Stage
University of California
Oakland, California, United States

APPENDIX 2
TEST DEVELOPMENT TEAM

Australian Council for Educational Research (ACER)	**National Institute for Educational Measurement (CITO)**
Margaret Wu Co-ordinator, ACER Test Development	Steven Bakker Co-ordinator, CITO Test Development
Jan Lokan	Bart Bossers
Joy McQueen	Karin Bugel
Juliette Mendelovits	Truus Dekkers
Gayl O'Connor	Ico De Roo
	Kees Lagerwaard
	Erna Van Hest
	Gerben van Lent